SPELLS DEATH

The authors of this book take the reader step by step through five homicide investigations that happened in Toronto during the nineteen seventies. These stories are the cases of Detective William McCormack, retired Chief of Police from the time period that he spent with the Toronto Police Homicide Squad … but this is more than just a book of facts.

Throughout the chapters, there is an intertwining of the two authors, father and daughter – both Toronto cops – during different time periods. Several cases hold common denominators and common criminals. The building of relationships through a devastating time period is explored and the events that would change the lives of several people, including an idealistic teenager chronicled.

The five cases cover tales of serial killers, cop killers and the intimate perspective provided by those who see death and destruction from the other side. This book delves into the investigations and the frustrations of the "system" that sometimes fails to deliver.

"10-45"
SPELLS DEATH

"10-45"
SPELLS DEATH

by

Kathy McCormack Carter

with

William J. McCormack

White Knight Publications
Toronto, Canada

Published in 2004 by White Knight Publications,
a division of Bill Belfontaine Ltd.
Suite 103, One Benvenuto Place
Toronto Ontario Canada M4V 2L1
T. 416-925-6458 F, 416-925-4165
E-mail whitekn@istar.ca
Web site: www.whiteknightpub.com

Ordering information
CANADA   UNITED STATES
Hushion House Publishing Inc.   Hushion House Publishing Inc.
c/o Georgetown Terminal Warehouses   c/o Stackpole Distribution
34 Armstrong Avenue,   7253 Grayson Road
Georgetown ON, L7G 4R9   Harrisburg PA, 17111 USA
T:1-866-485-5556 F:1-866-485-6665   T:1-888-408-0301 F: 1-717-564-8307

National Library of Canada Cataloguing in Publication
Carter, Kathy McCormack
        10-45 spells death / Kathy McCormack Carter.

ISBN 0-9734186-5-6
1. Murder—Ontario—Toronto—Investigation. 2. McCormack, William, 1933-.
3. Carter, Kathy McCormack. 4. Murder—Ontario—Toronto.
I. Title. II. Title: Ten forty-five spells death.
HV6535.C33T67 2004a   363.2'59523'09713541   C2004-903267-4

Cover and text design: Karen Petherick, *Intuitive Design International Ltd.*
Cover photos: Kathy McCormack Carter, Karen Petherick, the Irwin Family
Typeset in: Janson
Editing: Bill Belfontaine

Printed and bound in Canada

The following product and company names appearing in the book are trademarks
or trade names of their respective companies: Coke and Coca-Cola.

For Bailey and Madeline

ACKNOWLEDGEMENTS

As with any book, there are many people who assist with interviews, research, files and donate their time in the flesh or in spirit. To all of the following, I thank you from the bottom of my heart.

Staff Inspector Bob Clarke, Detective Scott Bronson, Toronto Police Homicide Squad

Constable Kevin Demoe, Constable Steve Harrigan, Toronto Police

Superintendent Ken Cenzura, Toronto Police

Detective Steve Skerret, Halton Regional Police

Staff Inspector Gary Ellis, Toronto Police

Sergeant Don Madigan, Toronto Police (retired)

Detective Jack Sutton, Hamilton Police (retired)

His Honor, Justice Michael Moldaver, Ontario Appellant Court, Osgoode Hall

A special thanks to:

Barb and Stephen Irwin, a true part of who I am today.

Staff Superintendent Jack Webster (retired, deceased) who gave me confidence to write.

Staff Sergeant Chuck Konkel Toronto Police, friend, writer, editor.

Detective Sergeant Mark Collins,
Ontario Provincial Police who continues to spur me on.

Bill Belfontaine my editor and publisher

My life lines: Ruta Delzotto, Maire Johnston,
Donna Glanfield, Nanette O'Connor, Vanessa Ward,
Karen Santer, Michelle Scorrano, Teresa D'Agostino,
Maureen Madigan, aka "The Girls Club."

The members of Whitby OPP Detachment,
especially my team, "A" platoon,

Maxwell ...

Bill and Jodi, Mike and Liz, Jamie and Tracey, Lisa,
remember I love you and believe in you all;
we shall endure and thrive,

My mom Jean, Dad of course, Rose and Fraser,
Bill and Debbie,

And the two angels on my shoulder ...
Margaret McCormack and Minnie Nelson.

CONTENTS

FOREWORD

That particular February morning in Toronto was exceptionally crisp and cold. A light dusting of snow had settled over the frozen ground adding a fresh, new appearance to the hardened frost that had accumulated over the past month. Sunday morning, quiet, peaceful, serene. The runner left his home with his dog for a routine sprint. Little did he know, this was to be the run of his life.

It began as usual, running through the park he had known for years. Daylight breaking, his breath shot out in front of him in long columns of steam. The only sound was the crunching of his shoes as each step landed on the snow-covered terrain. He was halfway through the solitude of the barren trees when he stopped dead in his tracks. The legs, stiff, white, uncovered, protruding from what appeared to be the top of a makeshift wooden bin. He shook his head. Was he mistaken? Was it just a mannequin, a leftover prank? Driven by curiosity, he drew closer, calling out to his dog to come away from it. The dog ignored him, continuing to sniff and dig frantically.

"Get away from there Sam," he called nervously, moving closer a step at a time until he was near enough to peer into the bin. The dog continued to dig. Then he saw her – the partially nude body lying face down, a few dead leaves swirling around her. His stomach churned, bile rose to his throat and he leaned over to vomit up his breakfast. He'd never seen this type of death. Straightening, he kicked at the snow, burying the contents of his stomach. Grabbing the dog's leash, he turned and ran towards home.

"Call the cops," he muttered, "got to call the cops."

* * *

A single decade can bring about many changes that often appear unnoticed. We find ourselves caught up in day-to-day living, work, school, friends and family without noticing the subtle transformation of moment and time. Acquaintances come and go, couples get married, divorced, have kids. Kids grow up. People die.

Day by day, week-to-week, we fail to notice change until it's left behind us, just a memory to be re-visited, often at strange times. Most change is slow and methodical, allowing the subconscious to adjust gradually and accept it unconditionally. It is that instant change that when it is thrust upon us, can be the most difficult to accept.

With every change, comes a degree of wisdom. Age usually brings this realization, a realization we don't hold close or even recognize when we are young. We learn so much from making a single change, just one decision. The one sure thing in life is nothing remains the same.

The seventies was a time of great change for many people. The war in Vietnam finally came to an end for the American military. Elvis Presley, the King of Rock and Roll would at last give up the fight to stay alive after changing the music scene forever. Tie-dye was in, fat ties and striped pants were commonplace for the modern man in the business world. Charlie's Angels ruled the television set with the famed Farrah Fawcett haircut becoming all the rage and where was I? Right smack in the middle of it. In this single decade, I would move from being a child to an adult, starting the decade out as a student in grade four to finishing it as one of a handful of female cadets with the Metropolitan Toronto Police Force.

That was a decade that brought unwelcome change for so many people whose lives were touched either directly or indirectly by tragedy – especially murder! It was also a time of intense struggle and investigation for my father who at the time was a Staff Sergeant in the Toronto Police Homicide Squad. He dedicated his police career in the 1970s to solving these crimes.

I turned sixteen in 1976, immersed in grade eleven studies at Notre Dame High School in the "Upper Beaches" area of Toronto. I had the world in the palm of my hand. My biggest challenge was to keep from getting kicked out of gym class. I stumbled through my teenage years as did many, fighting against what I knew to be right and wrong, drugs, sex, alcohol, all the temptations that every teen faces and at the start, I was a shy, small kid. I was one of the smallest in my grade nine class. I entered highschool at five feet two inches, one hundred and four pounds and left grade twelve five foot eight, one hundred and thirty. During those years, I gained confidence daily with the assistance of my closest friends, Michelle, Maire, Nanette, Teresa, Karen and Donna.

By grade eleven, I was outspoken, the class clown, ready for anything. All anyone had to do was dare me! The nuns who taught me were never impressed with my antics and made a point of advising my parents on several occasions.

Busily making my way through high school and having the time of my life, I was sure that I could get away with anything on a dare or not. My father was a Homicide Detective who worked most nights, and my Mom belonged to Church groups and socials that took her out in the evening. This of course, allowed me more freedom than my friends received. At sixteen, I was totally ignorant of what my father's job entailed. I knew he was a cop, a fact that didn't make me all that popular with my friends. We drank underage at local bars, smoked cigarettes, most of which, I took from the top of Dad's dresser then having to spend a good deal of time and effort trying to cover my tracks so he wouldn't find out. Little did I realize with his eye for detail and his most unusual memory, he never missed a thing.

It was only years later that I realized how naive I had been. There I was, a teenager thinking that all it took to hide the smell of alcohol or tobacco was a tic-tac popped into my mouth before I walked in the side door. I just knew he'd never suspect. Why would he bother when he was out solving the most complex of crimes, Homicide. He was making sense of life and death and I thought I was fooling him with a breath mint!

Less than a decade later, I was a rookie police officer on the Toronto Police Force. By the time I joined in 1980, my dad had been promoted to Inspector and moved out of the Homicide Squad after a stint from 1970 to the end of 1979. When I was a kid, he didn't talk about his cases much. I remember several instances where he came home from work after being gone forty-eight hours straight, marching upstairs, showering until the hot water ran out, then returning downstairs with his suit, tie, shirt and underwear in a green garbage bag, sealed and ready for the trash. He could never wear the clothes again after being at the scene of a rancid death. I never realized how the stench could permeate material and trigger the mental image of the scene on the first whiff.

It is only after experiencing twenty years of police work that I truly understand what he went through. The stench of rotting flesh that lingers in your nostrils and clings to your clothes, hours and sometimes days after leaving a death scene where decomposition had set in after a body remained undiscovered for an extended period of time. The flies, bugs and maggots that are so much nature's component of the putrid scenes of death, instantly cause a flip of even the strongest stomach and an itch to the skin of the observer. But it was always the smell that invaded the senses so completely, forever haunting.

My father kept many items of fact of his cases from that ten year period of the nineteen seventies. The small pieces of complex puzzles, the files, pictures, TV guides with notes scrawled on them, notes made in blood. He even kept a can of Coca-Cola, that would show up fifteen years later in the most unique situation. In the mid-eighties, my youngest sibling, Lisa, was introducing us to her new boyfriend Vince who had come to the house for dinner. My family are a tough bunch, loving but protective, especially when it came to the baby of the family. There are five in all, Bill Jr. is the eldest, then me, Mike, Jamie and Lisa. All, except Lisa and my mom are Police Officers. My sister's new boyfriend sat nervously at the dining room table while we scrutinized him mercilessly.

"Would you like something to drink?" my mom asked, noting beads of perspiration over his eyebrows.

"A Coke, if you have one," Vince answered politely.

"Humm," Mom sighed, then her eyes lit up, "I'll be back in a minute."

There was no pop in the fridge, but she had seen one in

the basement while doing the laundry. She took the stairs two at a time and returned triumphantly, Coca-Cola in hand.

"Here you are," she said, placing the can in front of him.

"Thanks," he smiled, then said, "this is strange." as he began to fiddle with the top of the can, "I haven't seen one of these in years."

We thought the kid had cracked up. Hadn't seen a Coke in years? What rock had he been hiding under?

Slowly, all eyes on him, he brought the can to his lips. A torrent of sticky brown liquid spewed from his mouth in a great funnel as he coughed and choked, thinking for sure that Mom killed him. It was like acid. Closer inspection revealed that Vince wasn't too far off when he said he hadn't seen a Coke like that in years. It had a foil type closure that was shaped in a triangle. A small band of aluminum adhesive sealed the rows of tiny holes that once peeled back, were sure to let through only the right amount of liquid at every gulp. Coca-Cola stopped making this pull top can in the early seventies! It was only later that we learned this particular can had been a key piece of evidence in a murder case my dad had investigated, a case where the murderer, after stabbing his victim to death, went to the fridge to get a drink. After selecting the can, the murderer thought better of it. He buried it deep inside the fridge, thinking no one would ever know. He was so sure no one would ever find it, he didn't wipe his fingerprints from it. Casually, he strolled out of the kitchen.

Thankfully for me, most of the memoirs Dad kept were in written form and of great assistance in providing stunning details that make this book so unusual.

I find it interesting that human lives are so intertwined. Many of us share common bonds, a person, a place, an item. Almost all of the cases in this book contain names and memories of police officers both my father and I worked with and are proud to call friends. We shared police stations, patrolled the same streets, encountered the same officers at one time or another throughout our careers, and, even had dealings with a killer we both came across, years apart.

I continue my work as a police officer and still seek my father's advice when dealing with day-to-day cases. It is a new decade, a century of new criminal and law enforcement advances. I never know what change will affect me next, but I do know that reflection on the past makes me a better officer, a better investigator and a better person.

My father remains a gentleman, an icon, a man I admire more than words could ever describe. His legacy lives on within the policing community, province-wide, Canada-wide and for that matter internationally. It is with great pride that I join with him to pass on some of his greatest achievements and knowledge to you.

The author and her father, ex-chief of police,
William McCormack.

Murder

"The unlawful killing of a human being with malice aforethought."

My Father, Detective Herman Lowe and two uniform officers
taking notes in the hallway at the murder scene.

CHAPTER ONE

DOUGLAS LAWRENCE MCCAUL

IN MARCH 1987, the stone-faced building housing the officers of 53 Division was located on the northwest corner of Yonge Street and Montgomery Avenue, just north of Eglinton Avenue, in the upper section of downtown Toronto. It was a typical style police station with tons of old Toronto character. It looked very much like a New York City precinct with cement steps leading up to the heavy oak front doors.

A sign hung over the door clearly visible in every type of Toronto weather. This station had been around for over fifty years and the more senior cops referred to it as the old "Twelve Division." It was Dad's second home as a Detective from 1967 to 1968. I also spent two years there. In 1988, the officers of 53 Division packed up and physically moved two blocks southwest into a modern building on Eglinton Avenue West and Duplex Avenue. This left the old building vacant and since that time, it has been used for the filming of countless movies and TV shows depicting police life.

The old 53 Division had the look and feel of a true police station. The front doors were so heavy to move that they had to be heaved open. In the wintertime, this allowed the wind and snow to blow through to the front office whenever anyone entered. A large, round wooden counter separated all officers from the public and a narrow staircase led the way up to the detective offices.

The public used the front door. To the west, in what we considered the rear was a sally port (another word that I learned upon induction to the police force. It simply meant a garage) adjacent to a fire hall. It held three garage openings where two cars fit snuggly in each and a side door that led directly into the cell area of the division. This was the officers' entrance. It was also the way most prisoners entered and exited. The upstairs detective office was a large room, manned with twelve desks that faced each other. One of the officer's had brought in an old radio that crackled out the tunes of a local station. Clouds of cigarette smoke lingered close to the ceiling, high-lighted by the florescent lights. A pot of coffee was always brewing in the corner, half empty mugs or Styrofoam cups littered the tops of the desks.

The entire building was heated by steam radiators that were hot to the touch and extremely noisy when they did function.

* * *

I was twenty-five years old and had been on the job for six years when in February 1986, I was transferred from 43 Division, an eastern Scarborough location to 53 Division in the upper Toronto area. I was a uniformed patrol officer at that time and I settled in comfortably. I met my husband that year. March 24, 1987 had turned out to be a great day! It was my mom's birthday and Max and I were getting engaged. All was pretty much right with my world.

I was working midnights, the graveyard shift (11:00 p.m. to 7:00 a.m.) with my partner John Manning who was more fondly known as "The Duke." It was a fairly quiet night and in the winter, Tuesday nights on the beat are not overly exciting. At about 1:25 a.m., I investigated a female at Yonge Street and Merton Street. Having checked her with the dispatcher, I found out that she owed seven hundred dollars in warrants so I placed her under arrest and brought her into the station.

The second floor detective office was buzzing. Several plainclothes officers, as well as uniformed guys smoked cigarettes, drank coffee and banged away proficiently with two fingers on Underwood typewriters. Marching through the office, prisoner in tow, I said hello to everyone, enjoying the ambiance of this well-oiled machine.

Sitting behind an empty desk, I pulled out my memo book and began to write up the information on the female I had brought into the office. One phone call and her sister was on the way to bail her out. Lucky for her. We didn't have bank machines in 1987 and finding someone with seven hundred dollars cash at that time of the morning was a near miracle! As I wrote, I noticed a small man, shabbily dressed, seated on a wooden chair beside the desk of Sergeant Mike Luxton. Mike was a big man who ran the Detective office in the absence of the Staff Sergeant. We still called it the "D" office even though the rank of Detective had been taken away in the early

seventies by Chief Adamson and not re-instated until my
father became Chief of Police.

The man's name was Douglas McCaul. He smiled at me
and I returned to what I was doing. Detectives Steve Harrigan
and Kevin Demoe were two plain-clothes officers in 53
Division who hovered over the little guy in the chair. A second
look told me that there was nothing to involve me. Male,
white, in his early thirties. He looked scrawny, probably from
missing too many meals. Then he crossed his legs and fidgeted
nervously as the officers continued their paperwork.

"Bill McCormack was the best cop I ever knew. Call him,
get him down here. I want to talk to him," said the scrawny guy.

I raised my eyes from my memo book thinking he was
talking to me but he hadn't glanced in my direction. He was
focused on Mike Luxton.

"Yeah, how's that?" Mike asked.

"He's the one who arrested me for murder," the scrawny
guy replied. That caught my attention.

"What ever happened to him, doesn't he still work here?"

"He's a bigwig downtown now," Mike responded, typing
furiously. "Matter of fact, that's his daughter over there." Mike
lifted his eyes, stopped typing and pointed a finger in my
direction.

I couldn't believe it! He had just told this murderer who I
was!

"Really? Bill McCormack is your dad?" the murderer
asked, turning his full attention to me.

"Yeah," I answered bluntly. I didn't want to give out more
information than that.

"Your dad is the nicest cop I ever met."

"Glad to hear it," I snapped back.

"No, I mean it." He leaned forward in his chair as if to
close the distance.

"He treated me really good. His partner Herman Lowe, I didn't like him. I wouldn't tell him anything, but your dad is a true gentleman. He always gave me a smoke when I wanted one, and a cup of coffee."

My father and Herman Lowe had been partners in the homicide squad for over five years. "Herm" as Dad called him, was a great guy. He'd died of cancer that very week.

This was nothing I hadn't heard before, but usually it was from other officers that I welcomed accolades about my father. He always treated people fairly and with respect. He never forgot a name and would take the time to say hello to everyone.

"How'd you meet my dad?" I asked, skeptical of where the murderer was trying to take the conversation. Either the guy was lying or exaggerating, after all, everyone my dad arrested would be still in jail, at least that's what I thought.

McCaul leaned back, drifting off somewhere deep in his own thoughts. I watched him closely. He was a slight man, five feet six would be stretching it and he may have weighed about one hundred and twenty pounds. I was two inches taller. Suited up in my full uniform, gun belt and all, I outweighed him by a good fifteen pounds. He seemed timid, not threatening in the least, as a matter of fact, I thought he looked sick, emaciated. I hadn't noticed his eyes at first but when I looked closer, I saw it. His eyes were like two dark pools, hollow, holding nothing. He appeared to look right through me.

McCaul smiled again. He was back. "I killed three people. Your dad got me for two. I really had him going for a while there. He never did get me for the third one though." He paused, waiting for my reaction. I made sure I showed nothing, yet I still decided to bite.

"Three murders?" I asked, "Who did you kill?"

"Couple of girls and a guy. Never did get me for the third one." He sat back.

"Why's that?" I asked, hoping to find the missing link, solve the long lost crime.

"He couldn't find the knife." McCaul whispered, cupping his hand to his mouth as if to prevent the other officers from hearing.

"Really?" I pondered. "So where was it?"

"Don't matter now, does it?"

"I guess not." How likely would it be that he would give me a key piece of evidence right here in this police station? "This guy been advised of his rights?" I asked Harrigan.

"Oh yeah," Steve told me. "He's going back to St. Thomas tonight."

"Ah, the psychiatric hospital." I nodded knowingly. There had to be something substantial in a person's background if they had been sent to St. Thomas Hospital.

"Your dad was good. I had him going for a while there though. Got a smoke?" he asked.

The stains between his right index and middle finger showed he was a chain smoker.

"Nope, sorry."

He shrugged his shoulders. "You know he found my identification at the scene."

"Really?" I asked. First I'd heard of this story. I couldn't figure the guy out. Was he telling the truth? I'd had enough and got up to leave.

"You tell your father that Doug McCaul was asking for him," he shot after me.

"I'll do that." The guy gave me the creeps, a little too weird for my liking.

I left the arresting officers to their job.

Steve Harrigan followed me out of the office. "He really

did kill a couple of people you know," he said as we reached the top of the stairs.

"How did you get him?" I asked in amazement, I couldn't believe a three-time murderer was out on the streets.

"You won't believe this one!" Steve laughed and told me the story.

* * *

I

Steve and Kevin were working together on the night of March 24th, 1987. They were in plainclothes and assigned to patrol the residential area north of Eglinton Avenue, east of Yonge Street, where there had been a rash of break and enters. They worked undercover in a brown Toyota Corolla. It was a cool, still night. At 1:00 a.m., they were northbound on Mount Pleasant Road, passing Broadway Avenue when Steve observed a male rider turn his motorcycle into the lot of a closed gas station located at the southwest corner of Mount Pleasant Road and Erskine Avenue. At the same time, a call went out over the police radio for all units advising them to return to the Division for immediate information on a wanted party.

"Should we go in?" Steve asked.

"In a minute," Kevin replied. "I want to watch this guy for a bit."

The male was driving a red motor scooter; a black helmet covered his face. He got off the scooter and parked it between two parked cars in the gas station lot. The station had been closed for hours. Immediately, he got back on the bike and just sat there.

"This looks interesting," Steve remarked.

"Yeah, let's watch him. Park the car," Kevin answered. Steve turned the car left on Erskine Avenue, shut off the headlights and traveled halfway down the block before turning around to come back. They parked facing east, approximately a hundred feet from the gas station. This gave them full view of the suspect without revealing their location. The driver got off the bike keeping his helmet on. He walked south toward the kiosk and opened the door to the washroom. The door was open, there was a small glass window at the top. He went out of sight but returned after a couple of seconds and walked back to the bike. While he was in the washroom, Steve noticed that he did not turn the light on.

"Strange," he muttered to his partner.

"Wonder what he's up to?" Kevin asked.

McCaul walked back to where his bike was parked and then suddenly ducked down behind a car for about five seconds, attempting to hide himself from something or somebody, and then he stood up, got on the bike and drove quickly off the lot without looking back.

"Here he comes." Steve whispered.

"Yup, let's go."

The officers got ready to follow McCaul as he proceeded westbound on Erskine Avenue, unknowingly passing the police car.

Steve pulled a U-turn, keeping his distance. They followed the bike to Redpath Avenue. McCaul turned right and went north on the dead-end street.

"Shit, it's a dead end," Steve muttered.

"Just drive by him." Kevin wasn't worried, their cover wasn't blown yet.

The officer's drove past. McCaul turned the bike around and went south. As he came up to the intersection of Redpath

and Erskine again, he quickly made another U-turn and went
back up the dead end street.

"Now what?" Steve asked.

"Pull into someone's driveway," Kevin directed.

He swung the car into the driveway and turned the lights
off. McCaul parked the bike at the end of the street and got
off, still wearing his helmet. He was walking north. To the
north of this location is a small park and a parking lot. Steve
and Kevin got out of the car. Heading towards him, Steve
yelled: "Hey you! Stop, It's the Police!"

McCaul turned back startled and started to run. After a
short chase, they had him. Both officer's pulled out their
badges and identified themselves.

"Why did you run?" Steve asked, catching his breath, one
hand held tightly around McCaul's arm.

McCaul took off the helmet. He wanted to be heard cor-
rectly. "You were following me!"

"Where do you live?" Steve asked.

"Nowhere. I have no fixed address."

Steve took one arm and Kevin the other and walked him
back to his bike. A red Honda Elite motor scooter.

"Do you have any identification?" Kevin asked.

"Here's my driver's license." McCaul pulled an Ontario
Driver's license, complete with picture from the back pocket
of his jeans and handed it to Kevin.

"I'll check it out." Kevin nodded to his partner. He
retrieved the portable radio from the inside of his jacket
pocket and made the call to the dispatcher.

Steve turned again to McCaul. "Where do you live?" he
repeated his question.

"In St. Thomas. I just came to Toronto to visit." McCaul
stared at his feet.

"What were you doing at that gas station?"

"Nothing. I just used the washroom. The officers remained silent, starring intently at him, awaiting further comment. "Okay, okay … if you check, I'm AWOL from St. Thomas Psychiatric Hospital."

Steve was surprised but concealed it. St. Thomas Psychiatric. He must have done something pretty serious to get in there. "What did you do to be sent to the Psychiatric Hospital?"

Without hesitation McCaul answered the question. "In 1976 I killed a woman and I buried her just up there in Muir Park," pointing north. Steve had worked at 53 Division for a number of years. He vaguely remembered a case like that.

"Are you the guy who left his Driver's license at the scene of the body?" he asked disbelievingly.

"No. The police found my identification not my license beside the body."

"He's wanted on a Lieutenant Governor's warrant," Kevin yelled to Steve, hearing the dispatcher's response from his check. "McCaul, you're under arrest!"

Placing him under arrest, the officers advised him of his rights to counsel and cautioned him against saying anything to them. They performed a physical search and asked him to open the small trunk portion of his bike. McCaul produced a small key and unlocked the trunk. Steve found pornographic magazines, two pairs of women's shoes and various pieces of ladies underwear and clothing.

"That's my transvestite clothes. You can't charge me for having that!" McCaul scoffed.

"We won't," Steve assured.

"Where are you taking me?" McCaul asked.

"We'll take you into the office and see what's going on," Kevin answered.

"Can you take me to my mother's house? She lives around

here. You can take me to Penetang, just don't take me back to St. Thomas. I don't like it there."

"Let's go," Steve said. He made sure the bike was locked before loading McCaul into the back seat of the car. Within five minutes they were sitting behind their desks.

"And you know what the weirdest part of this is?" Steve folded his arms in front, leaning against the wall in the hallway, waiting for my response.

"Hey, nothing shocks me anymore," I replied, shaking my head.

"McCaul was originally in Penetanguishene Mental Hospital. He was sent there in 1976 for life after a murder he committed here. Then, he was transferred to St. Thomas on a Lieutenant Governor's warrant. The provisions for the warrant were changed in 1986 when he was allowed full absence from the hospital with conditions. I guess he breached the conditions tonight so they revoked them and listed him as an escapee. Best part of this is that he actually gets a loan from the Credit Union across the street from the Psychiatric Hospital to buy his little scooter. Then he fucks off on it and drives to Toronto. Beat that. The guy's a two time murderer, and, the information the dispatcher was having all officers return to the station to be made aware of was that it was McCaul who was the escapee they should be on the lookout for."

As it turned out, McCaul didn't just drive straight to Toronto. He'd made a stop in Burlington that would result in another charge against him. One of attempted murder. And, McCaul had been living a life of leisure for a two-time killer from St. Thomas. He'd been transferred from the Oak Ridges Center in Penetanguishene to St. Thomas in 1981 and was granted a full time pass from the hospital in October 1986. The provisions for his newfound freedom included that he maintain full employment, reside in a boarding house on

Chester Street and that he report to the hospital on Mondays as well as keeping a daily log of his activities. He got a nice little part-time job at a local restaurant called "Wellington Court" in the town of St. Thomas where he worked as an assistant cook.

The loan for his Honda Scooter was for a total of twenty-four hundred dollars and he was making monthly payments from his little income. Never one to stay out of trouble, he began making obscene phone calls to a woman in St. Thomas and later disclosed the three murders to a female cab driver when he had taken a cab ride. Once again the police came knocking.

A year after he was given his leave of absence, the hospital decided to change his conditions. They demanded that he return to the hospital and only be allowed to go out each day to his job at the restaurant. But, McCaul was getting nervous. He knew the review board wouldn't look lightly at his latest brushes with the law and would most likely keep him in St. Thomas or move him back to Penetanguishene.

After reeling him in somewhat, the common practice at the hospital was for the nurses to hand him the keys to his bike fifteen minutes before he was to start work. If he didn't show up at the restaurant, his employer would call the hospital. When he failed to show up at work at 4:00 p.m. on the evening of March 24, 1987, the hospital was notified and the Lieutenant Governor's warrant was re-instated. A telex message to arrest McCaul on sight was sent out to all police forces across Ontario.

St. Thomas is a quaint little town in Southwestern Ontario. The closest city to it is London and the next town over, Aylmer, is home to the Ontario Police College. This is where new recruits from all parts of Ontario train to become full-fledged police officers. Douglas Lawrence McCaul was making one more trip before they pulled in the reins for good. He was on a mission to get to Toronto.

It was a clear afternoon with a chill breeze that was consistent with the remnants of winter that often held on into late March. The most direct route to Toronto from St. Thomas is Highway 76 north to Highway 401 east. Not much of a problem if you're driving a car, however, it's a whole different ball game with a scooter. The bike couldn't reach the type of speeds needed to keep up with other vehicles on the highway and so he decided to take the back roads.

Instead of going to work, McCaul put a pair of blue jeans over his white work pants, pulled on a blue nylon spring jacket, stuffed the sleeves with green garbage bags and got out his blue motto-cross gloves and scooter.

He was ready to go. The trip took time, but he made his way slowly, methodically. It was just after 7:00 p.m., not quite dark when he got to the Super Center on Guelph Line in Burlington. Parking the Honda in the lot, helmet locked to the bike, he pulled out his smokes and placed one in his mouth. Inhaling deeply, he looked around the lot. Lots of time.

Judy Hensch was in a hurry. It had been a long day. After paying for the groceries, she loaded them up on the cart, two cases of Coke on the underside, and made her way to the parking lot. Just another component of her usual routine. Arriving at her car, she took the keys out and opened the trunk. It only took a few minutes to put the bags in and she decided there wasn't enough room for the pop. The two cases would have to go in the passenger side of the car. She placed her purse inside the trunk before slamming it securely.

Maneuvering the cart between the two parked cars was a little more difficult, but Judy was able to lift the cases and place them in the front seat. The Super Center has a specific area in the middle of the parking lot for empty carts and Judy returned hers dutifully before returning to her car. A man passed by, but she paid him no attention. Keys in hand, she opened the driver's door. In a split second, McCaul ran around the front of her car directly behind her and pushed her into the driver's seat.

"Get into the car!" he ordered.

Judy screamed, a shrill screech that attracted the attention of another woman walking through the lot.

"Get into the fucking car!" The man was fanatical, wild, pushing with his left hand, holding something else in his right.

Judy's response was instant, unexpected to this maniac. Thinking quickly, she remembered she had a weapon, her car keys. She struck at her assailant, twice coming close to his left eye. Then she saw it, dread filled her body. The knife came up swiftly, with precision. She screamed again.

"Shut the fuck up!"

She felt the knife reach its mark, once, twice. "Escape, get the hell out of there." It was the only thing Judy could think of to do. She dove in the car, feeling the knife once again strike the back of her leg. She made it. Locking the door, she sounded the horn, laying on it. The man ran. The last thing he wanted was attention.

Not knowing how bad she was hurt, Judy just wanted to get away, get out of the parking lot. She drove away, frantically searching for someone to help. She stopped at the first couple she saw coming out of the store.

"I have to get out of here, a man stabbed me!" Judy cried to the horrified couple.

The woman looked at her in disbelief.

"Call the Police." Judy screamed. She hit the gas, afraid he was right behind her. Petrified, she drove home. Her husband would know what to do. When she arrived, Judy knew she had to get to a hospital, but first they called the police. Constable

Peter McAlpine of Halton Regional Police was the first officer
to respond. He took Judy to the hospital along with Detectives
Dickie and Gardener. Judy was able to describe her attacker
and the officers made arrangements for her to attend at Police
Headquarters to provide details of the attacker to a police
artist.

Judy's wounds required several stitches. Shakily, she
accompanied the police officers to headquarters where
Constable Amis was waiting. With Judy's help, they put
together a composite that would be released to the media and
other officer's in the region. That day, the injured woman
returned home, changed forever.

McCaul, on the other hand, got back on his scooter and
headed east. He had to make a few more stops that night.
During his stay in St. Thomas, he'd made friends with some
of the other inmates and got to know some of the day patients
who were not there for criminal reasons. One of these friends
had been released earlier and was living in Toronto. Marjorie
Clements had a bad feeling about Doug McCaul when she
met him in St. Thomas. He was known to be dangerous and
she was nervous around him. Marjorie now had a boyfriend
who was taking treatment at Queen Street Mental Health
Clinic in Toronto. On March 24, 1987 at approximately 9:05
p.m., she left the clinic in her car and started driving home.

Marjorie drove east on Queen Street, to Victoria Street.
At the red traffic light, a small motorcycle pulled up beside her
and the driver waved. At first, she didn't pay attention to him,
thinking he must be waving at someone else, then, the driver
took off his helmet. It was Douglas McCaul. Now what?
Marjorie pulled over into a gas station lot off Queen Street
and he came to the car.

She opened the driver's window slightly. "I didn't know

you were out?" Marjorie questioned, trying her best to hide her trepidation.

He leaned against the car. It was dark outside, but the area was well lit. He smiled mischievously. "I'm not. I took off. Mind if I get in?" He walked around the front of the car, not taking his eyes off Marjorie. The passenger door was unlocked. He opened the door and sat on the seat, both legs hanging out the side with the door ajar.

"You know those doctors in St. Thomas keep telling me I'm a killer." Doug told her. Marjorie didn't know what to say. She changed the subject.

"Why did you come to Toronto?"

"I have to find a place to stay."

'I hope he doesn't think he's staying with me,' she thought.

He tapped his fingers against the window, noticeably nervous. The gas station attendant watched them from the kiosk. That gave Marjorie her way to get rid of him. "You know, you really should get going Doug. This is downtown Toronto. There are a lot of cops here. Maybe you should go outside the city and get a cheap hotel or something."

"Yeah, I would but all I got on me is thirty bucks. Maybe I can find an empty church or something to sleep in for the night. Then I'll turn myself in. I've got a few things I have to do still."

"That's a good idea." Marjorie sighed, openly relieved. "Better get going then."

"Yeah, see you around Marge."

"See you Doug."

He shut the door, helmet in hand and walked back to the bike, glaring at the attendant as he passed the kiosk.

Marjorie drove away, thankful that he hadn't pressed the matter of coming to her house. She looked in the rear-view mirror. The single light of the Honda shone brightly behind.

He was following her. Panicked, Marjorie turned onto the Don Valley Parkway and headed north. The parkway was a high-speed highway, she was sure to lose him there. North of Eglinton Avenue, Marjorie watched in her rear-view mirror as the bike veered off the exit ramp. He was gone! Thank God. She drove home as quickly as she could. But the night was still young for Douglas McCaul.

What to do? All this freedom, so little time. It could be snatched away from him at any second. He decided to go back downtown. The St. Charles Tavern was located on the west side of Yonge Street, south of Wellesley and was a well-known gay bar with two floors. The bottom floor had a bar and tables, the top floor was where patrons went to dance. The St. Charles was where Douglas McCaul made his next stop. Parking the bike in a lot across the street, McCaul went into the tavern to drink beer and talk to some of the gays.

All was well until a couple of uniformed foot patrol officers from 52 Division, Toronto's downtown police division, decided to do a routine check of the bar. It was his cue to leave. McCaul paid the tab, made his way out the front door onto the busy street where he could easily get lost in the crowd. Making his way south on Yonge Street, he crossed again and stood in front of the Zanzibar Tavern. The Zanzibar, known for it's tough clientele and female strippers was exactly opposite to the place he had just been in.

He was sure no one would notice him here. After all, it was dark, except for the stage. He took a seat at the back, next to the door. It went well until the police came in.

"Shit, they're everywhere!" he muttered to himself.

Time to get out of downtown Toronto. In a few minutes, he was back at the lot to reclaim his bike. Heading east again, he turned north on Jarvis Street and passed number 590, the Metropolitan Toronto Police Headquarters. Chuckling to himself, he thought of the many times he had been in that building, talking to Staff Sergeant McCormack and Sergeant Lowe. Didn't seem like that long ago. Making his way north on Mount Pleasant Road, he stopped one more time at a closed gas station, but this was not to be Douglas McCaul's lucky night. In a matter of moments, he would meet up with Constable Steve Harrigan and Constable Kevin Demoe who quickly put an end to his night of freedom.

II

McCaul's stops were not known to the arresting officers on the evening of March 24th 1987. He had covered a long distance, crossing several municipalities, regions and police jurisdictions. When Demoe and Harrigan were finished processing him, McCaul was transported back to St. Thomas by the Ontario Provincial Police who have jurisdiction throughout Ontario.

Arriving at last in the Hospital. McCaul was sure, he was home free. Detective Steve Skerrett and Detective Michael Kingston of the Halton Region Police Force, had other ideas.

March 25, 1987 was just another day for Skerrett. He'd been on the Halton Regional Police Force for eleven years and was attached to the Major Crime Bureau of the Regional Criminal Investigation Division. A seasoned veteran of eleven years, Steve had seen just about everything – homicide, suicide, theft and all manner of destruction. At approximately 11:20 a.m. that morning, Detective Skerrett was called to the Burlington Criminal Investigation Bureau to assist with an investigation.

He was given a copy of the report of the stabbing from the night before at the Super Center. Detective Mike Kingston and Detective Signey Pittman were assigned to the case. The three officers knew each other well.

"Who do we have for a suspect?" Steve asked after perusing the report.

Detective Kingston handed him a piece of paper. It was a "Zone Alert" issued the previous night with information on an escaped party from St. Thomas Psychiatric Hospital. The man named was Douglas McCaul. An in-depth description of McCaul, including his clothing was detailed on the alert. The words "CAUTION VIOLENT" got Steve's full attention.

"Here's what our victim had to say," Mike added, handing him Judy Hench's statement.

"Look's like this might be our boy," Steve murmured. Kingston nodded in agreement.

"I'll get a hold of St. Thomas. Do we have a videotaped statement from the victim?"

"Not yet," Detective Pittman answered. "We can do that today if you want."

"Yeah, that's a good idea. Do you want to make the arrangements to pick her up, Signey?"

"Sure. I'll look after it."

Detective Skerrett made the call. The hospital advised him that McCaul had been missing since about 3:45 p.m. the previous day but he had been returned to them by the Ontario Provincial Police that morning. They also told Detective Skerrett that McCaul had been arrested in Toronto about 1:00 a.m. by Constables Harrigan and Demoe of 53 Division. The hospital agreed to send a photograph to Skerrett.

Skerrett then reached Steve Harrigan. He was told about the arrest and given a description of McCaul. On Thursday March 26, 1987, Detective Skerrett received the picture of McCaul from the St. Thomas Psychiatric Hospital. The victim in the Super Center attack had provided a statement, as well as a composite drawing of the suspect. The picture and the composite were a close match. A trip to St. Thomas was next on the list.

On Friday March 27, 1987 Detective Skerrett and Detective Kingston drove to St. Thomas Psychiatric Hospital. Once there, they were allowed to view McCaul for themselves. It was evident that he matched the description of the suspect. Upon returning to the office, the two detectives interviewed a witness from the parking lot at the Super Center. She was shown the photograph the detectives carried and her immediate response was, "That's him!"

The evidence against McCaul was mounting. The detectives now had enough to gain a warrant for the arrest of Douglas McCaul on a charge of Attempt Murder. On Monday, March 30, 1987, warrant in hand, Skerrett and Kingston returned to St. Thomas. This time, they would be coming back with more than a picture.

McCaul came into the room where the two detectives were waiting.

"Douglas McCaul, do you know why we're here?" Detective Skerrett asked.

"Yeah, they told me about it." McCaul appeared resigned to what was coming.

"I want you to look at this." Skerrett showed him the warrant. "You are under arrest for Attempted Murder, do you understand?"

"Yeah."

"You have the right to retain counsel without delay."

"I already talked to my lawyer."

"Who is your lawyer?"

"Mr. Barry McKague. He works in Toronto."

"Okay, let's go." McCaul moved toward them. "Not without these." Skerrett dangled the handcuffs. There was no way this guy was going to walk to the car without his hands securely behind his back.

McCaul was taken back to the office in Halton where the detectives completed the paperwork and he was held overnight. In order for a proper identification to be made, Detective Skerrett contacted Metropolitan Toronto Police and spoke to Deputy Chief William McCormack. Arrangements were made to do an actual line-up at 52 Division the next day.

Constable Gary Ellis from 52 Division was assigned to the Criminal Investigation Bureau in plain-clothes. He was working on Tuesday, March 31, 1987 with his partner Sergeant Keith Rogers when he received a call from Detective Skerrett of the Halton Regional Police. Detective Skerrett requested that Constable Ellis assist in setting up a line-up for a suspect who had been arrested by Metro Toronto Police but was now charged with Attempted Murder in Halton Region. Gary Ellis was busy with his cases from the downtown area of Toronto but was more than willing to take the time to assist an officer from another jurisdiction.

Ellis and Rogers were given a description of the suspect. It was now their job to find similar looking candidates who would be willing to stand in the line-up. A tough task, but one they knew could be accomplished. Right away, they picked four police officers from 52 Division. Jim Wright, Gord Rasbach, Doug Peacock and Martin Woodhouse, all guys I had worked with. Rasbach had been my partner for a number of years. This was the easy part. It was far more difficult to get members of the general public to willingly be a part of a lineup. After all, who would want to take the chance to participate in an event that a victim might pick them out? Constable Ellis headed for the Bay Street Bus Terminal.

Within an hour, he had seven willing partakers, no monetary fee but a hot coffee and a meal.

By 3:50 p.m., the line-up was ready. Twelve suspects in all. Both the victim and an independent witness were led separately into the viewing room where they could view the twelve suspects through one-way glass. Both picked out McCaul. Skerrett had his man.

The trial for the attempted murder of Judy Hensch was held before a judge and jury. It commenced on January 18, 1988 and concluded three days later. The jury came back with a finding of 'Not Guilty'. All the facts had been presented and the case was fought valiantly by Crown attorney John Ayre, however, the witnesses had a much more difficult time with McCaul's identity now that he was seated in front of them clean shaven, sporting a tight haircut and wearing a suit and tie, a far cry from his disheveled, unshaven appearance on the night of the attack. After the trial ended, McCaul was returned to Penetanguishene Hospital on the Lieutenant Governor's warrant.

* * *

I was working the night shift on March 24, 1987, the night McCaul was arrested and brought to 53 Division. I was interested in hearing my dad's version of the story but had to wait until the morning. I didn't think he'd appreciate me calling and waking him up at 1:30 in the morning. After my shift ended at 7:00 a.m., I drove home after a most interesting night. Following a short sleep, I dialed the number at 40 College Street, the new location of Toronto Police Headquarters, where my father was one of three Deputy Chiefs of Police.

"Deputy Chief McCormack – Field Operations," he answered.

"Hi Dad."

"Hi honey, what's up?"

"Not too much, just woke up."

"Already? it's only eleven o'clock."

"I know, I couldn't sleep."

"Why not, what's up?"

"I wanted to tell you about a guy we had in the office last night."

"Oh yeah, who?"

"He told me you arrested him for murder." I had my Dad's full attention now.

"Really, what's his name?"

"Douglas McCaul," I answered. The line went silent. "Dad, you still there?"

"Are you sure?" he asked.

"Yeah, I'm sure. He was AWOL from St. Thomas. A couple of guys at 53 picked him up on a Lieutenant Governor's warrant."

Dad was dumbfounded. "I can't believe they let him out. Douglas McCaul is a very dangerous man. What the hell was he doing out?"

I related the story as Harrigan told it to me. Then, I got to the part where I met McCaul and he told me about the murders and the fact that they never got him for the third, due to the knife.

"He told you that?" he asked, shocked.

"Yeah, why?" I thought it was all common knowledge to him.

"I did find the knife. I sent it to the Center of Forensic Science but nothing came back. It had been wiped clean with bleach."

"Really? What exactly did he do? Who'd he kill?" I knew a fair amount about my dad's cases from the copies of files he kept. I often read through them because I was so fascinated with police investigative work.

"Douglas McCaul has a long history. I'll tell you what I know, here goes."

* * *

III

In 1976, I was a Staff Sergeant in the Homicide Squad and had been in the squad since 1968. In March of 1967, I had been promoted to Probationary Detective and was transferred from 52 Division to 53 Division. I was in 53 in 1968 when Detective Kevin Boyd shot and killed Angelo Nobrega. This was a huge case, the first real case that was ever looked at as an ethnic shooting involving a police officer. It was an accidental shooting that hit the media and they were relentless with it. Kevin was my partner for years before that and we were the best of friends. After the shooting, I was temporarily assigned to the Homicide Squad where I was the first probationary Detective ever so assigned. Back then you had to be a full-fledged Sergeant to get near this exclusive unit. I was working with Detective Sergeant George Thompson and Detective Wally Harkness.

In 1969, I was promoted to full Detective and officially transferred to the Homicide Squad. In 1975 I was promoted to Detective Sergeant and partnered with Sergeant Herman Lowe.

Lowe and I worked well together. He was a tough, no nonsense guy. What you saw was what you got with Herm. He was a great guy, a great detective and mostly a great friend. We investigated many, many cases together, but none that equaled Doug McCaul.

Sunday February 08, 1976 started out to be a normal day. I got up, took Jean, you and the other kids to church and was looking forward to getting home for a nice breakfast with the family. But it was not to be that day. Herm and I were on call and at 9:50 a.m. I got a phone call from Staff Sergeant Graham at Police Headquarters. A body had been found in Alexander Muir Park, which is located off St. Edmunds Avenue and Yonge Street. It was an affluent area of Northern Toronto.

I changed into a suit and tie and made my way to the scene, in my spiffy 1959 red and white two-seater Nash Metropolitan. Herman Lowe was already there when I arrived at 11:19 a.m. It was cold. The ground was frozen and there was a good amount of snow covering the topsoil. I was directed by two uniformed officers, Constable Karl Davis and Sergeant Lionel Gough to a trough-like compound heap located in the northeast corner of the park. Doctor James Ferris, the pathologist was called to the scene. He, along with Doctor J.D. Lovering, the on-call coroner and myself surveyed the scene.

It is important to note that it was my practice, especially at the scene of a difficult homicide, to notify the perspective pathologist in order that he or she would have a first hand observation of the body prior to the removal and to the conducting of a post-mortem examination. I find in many cases that this method is of scientific and pathological assistance to the findings later made by the pathologist.

It was then that I first saw the victim. She was lying face down, partially covered by snow and leaves. The body was in a compost heap, a square type of bin that was surrounded on three sides by railway ties, one piled on top of the other to form the sides. Upon closer inspection, we saw her legs. Her left leg was naked, a pair of black nylons were partially up the right leg. It appeared she had been there for a while, which was not surprising due to the fact that the body was well hidden and couldn't be seen from the street. There were footprints around the area in the snow and pieces of clothing scattered in the immediate area. It was imperative that the clothing at the scene not be disturbed until further minute cataloguing took place for the purpose of trace evidence – anything from loose hairs to scuff marks.

Alexander Muir Park is in the jurisdiction of 53 Division, the north end division that covers the Yonge/Lawrence area, so naturally they would have been notified first. Two 53 Division detectives were on the scene, Sergeant Edward Valois and Constable Robert Elliott. I looked around and noticed another guy in a suit. Inspector Rutledge McCormick Ryan was the duty Inspector. He was there by requirement of police procedure but stood back, observing only. As a former detective, he was well aware of the need not to contaminate the scene. He knew this had to be our show.

"Inspector," I called over to him. "It's nice to see you here. I could sure benefit from your experience at this scene. I'll be filing my report with you as soon as I can."

"Yeah Bill, I know, but you're on your own, I'm heading back to Headquarters."

With that, the Inspector left. We always had a mutual respect for each other.

"Okay, who found her?" I asked.

Constable Davis came forward. "Hi Staff, how's it going?"

"It was going okay until I got this call," I chuckled.

"Yeah, I know. Anyway, the guy who found her," Davis continued, "was out for an early morning jog with his dog. The dog wandered off and was sniffing at something over here in the trough. He tried to call the dog away but when it wouldn't come, he came to get it. That's when he saw her."

"Oh, I see, he had a body-sniffing dog, eh?"

Davis laughed. "Well Staff, I really don't think it was."

"Never mind, I was just kidding. Okay, where's that witness now?"

"He was pretty distraught. We got all his info and a statement and let him go home. Told him someone would be around to see him later."

"Good, did he touch anything?"

"Nope. Says he didn't."

"Okay. Let's get this scene under control before the media gets wind of it."

"Too late for that boss, look up there." Sergeant Valois walked over and pointed to the pavement at the top of the hill. The first of many reporters were hovering, taking in the scene, camera in hand.

"Okay Ed, do me a favor, go up and speak to the press and tell them we have a very difficult scene on our hands and advise them that my partner and I will be available as soon as we can to speak to them."

"I'm on it." Ed turned, scurrying up the hill to meet them.

"Sergeant Gough." The uniformed Sergeant came over to where I was standing.

"Yes sir."

"Set up a perimeter." I told him. "No media, no public. No one, including police officers, gets in or out of the scene without you knowing it and recording it."

"No problem Staff." Lionel Gough was a man who liked to take charge and he did so immediately, shouting orders into the portable radio he carried.

I looked up to see Ed Valois returning to the scene. "Spoke to the reporters, they're happy."

"Good, let's get the Emergency Task Force here. We could use them to search the area."

Ed nodded, then headed for the radio in the car. We didn't carry cellular phones back then.

"Staff Sergeant McCormack?" I turned around to find two more suits on the scene.

"Yeah?"

"Sergeant Tom Jeffery, along with Constable Doug Ford here. We're from Ident. What do you want us to do?"

"Hey guys, glad to have you." I shook hands. We had worked together before and these officers would be the identification officers who would carry the continuity throughout the investigation and the postmortem examination. "You know the routine, we'll start by collecting and photographing every piece of evidence. I'm just waiting for the coroner to pronounce her dead, then we'll get to work."

Doctor Lovering had no problem pronouncing death and the Identification Bureau guys went to work, photographing, collecting samples of blood from the snow around the body, bagging clothing, documenting evidence. With the help of Herman, the four of us turned the body on its back. I noticed that there was an imprint of ice in the snow outlining her chin and the sweater she was wearing. Doctor Ferris said that this was an indication that the body was placed in this position while still warm, the heat of her chin and chest melting the snow enough to leave the indentation.

Our victim was wearing a black turtleneck sweater and blue jean jacket. It was a difficult task removing her from the shallow grave. She was loaded onto a stretcher and placed inside a body bag, then removed from the scene and taken to the morgue where Herman and I would go after the initial investigation was complete.

In the meantime, there was work to be done. Sergeant

Ronald Route, Constable McCrorrie, Constable Doug Walker, Constable McKenzie and Constable Robert Johnston all arrived on the scene from the Emergency Task Force. A finer team, a homicide officer could not ask for. True professionals, all dressed in dark blue tactical police uniforms.

"Glad to see you guys." I thanked them for coming out.

"Glad to be of help," Sergeant Route answered. "What do you want us to do?"

"Let's start by assigning Constable Walker to be the recording officer. Anything anyone finds, he records where, when, what, you get the drift?"

Walker nodded his head. "And Doug, as for you, this isn't Vietnam, you're not in a gun ship or conducting a jungle patrol for the Vietcong, this is a very serious homicide investigation and I want you to realize that you are responsible to me, not the United States Government!"

Laughter erupted from Walker's comrades. Doug Walker was one of the few Canadians who enlisted in the United States Marine Corps and served two tours in Vietnam. He was a well-decorated soldier with a great sense of humor.

Doug saluted, holding his fingers tight to his head. "I accept the detail without question oh fearless Commander!"

I have often been questioned as to why we, as police officers, make jokes at the scene of something very serious. It is a difficult thing to explain to people but maintaining a sense of humor is paramount to ease the tension that surrounds this type of investigation. It is not meant in any way to make light of the situation, but death is not an easy thing for any human to deal with.

"Okay, back to business. Just so you know Staff, McCrorrie brought the metal detector," Route said.

"Good. We can use that. Put him to work."

"Right."

"As for Johnston, give him a rake, start working the area that was under the body. The rest of the guys can go through the immediate area but very slowly. Let's make this count. I want the surrounding area to the body searched to the ground and as far as we can get under the snow."

During this time, Herman was standing beside me, pen and notebook in hand. He was an excellent note taker – meticulous to a fault.

The Emergency Task Force officers worked diligently. It wasn't long before Constable Johnston came up with a key piece of evidence. He was raking the area under the body when he found a black folded leather wallet. It was embedded approximately three to five inches in the snow.

"BINGO!" Johnston picked the wallet up by the edges and examined it. It was a man's small billfold, on the lower left edge, the words "The *for ward* Line" were inscribed in gold. Inside the wallet was a Province of Ontario Birth Certificate in the name of Douglas Lawrence McCaul, a Department of Streets identification card, one Canadian five and one dollar bill. Constable Walker recorded the items. Constable Ford of the Identification Bureau photographed it, placed it in a clear plastic bag and handed it to Sergeant Lowe.

"Bill, the address for this guy is close by," Herm told me. "Want to pay him a visit?"

"Not yet. Let's see what we've got here first." Once we were done at the scene, our next step was the morgue to attend the autopsy that was scheduled for 1:00 p.m. I had to find out who the victim was so I had the guys from the Identification Bureau fingerprint the body at the morgue. I then detailed Sergeant Valois to check the missing persons reports.

It was 12:30 p.m. The scene was secure, one last detail before we left. I had to speak to the media. Herman and I walked up the hill. They were waiting patiently for any tidbit we could give them.

"Ladies and gentlemen, we are at the beginning of a very serious investigation."

"Is it a Homicide?" I recognized a Toronto Star reporter, the first to fire a question my way.

"Most likely, but I can't confirm it subject to the findings of the Post Mortem."

"Is the victim a male or female?" Toronto Sun.

"Female."

"How old?"

"Possibly thirties."

"How long has she been there Detective?" Now I had the TV camera in my face, the bright light temporarily blinding me.

"Possibly a few weeks, due to the weather conditions, the body is well preserved."

"Any suspects yet?"

"Now, you know I can't answer that, we're just starting this investigation."

They laughed.

"Detective," it was the Star reporter again, "can we get down there to take some pictures?" I could see he was straining the yellow police tape that Sergeant Gough had strung up.

"Not yet, the officers at the scene will give you clearance when they're finished, then you can shoot away. Now folks, my partner and I really have to get going."

"Just before you leave, can we get your names for the record?" They were writing furiously.

"Sure, Staff Sergeant Bill McCormack and Sergeant Herman Lowe, Homicide Squad, now if you will excuse us, we really have to go."

"Pack of wolves, eh?" Herm muttered as we made our way to the car.

"Yeah, but they have a job to do." I pulled out a pack of Winston's and gave one to Herm. We both lit up, inhaling deeply. Each scene you worked took a little something more from you.

"How did you get here?" I asked Herm.

"Came with the Inspector, I left my car at headquarters."

"Great, I'm parked right over there." I pointed to the Nash. Herman went white.

"Are you kidding? You want me to ride in that death trap?" Herman had been a mechanic before joining the Force and had grave misgivings about my prize possession.

"Come on, live a little." I said. "Just make sure you don't step too hard on the floor when you get in or we'll be traveling Flintstone style."

Herman climbed into the passenger seat and I got in behind the wheel. A couple of backfires and we were off, alerting the entire neighborhood. We headed towards Mount Pleasant Road, a direct route to the downtown morgue.

"Shit, Bill, does this thing have any heat?" Herm complained, rubbing his hands together.

"Never mind the heat, I'm starving. Missed breakfast, can you drop me at that little diner on Queen Street and I'll pick us up some burgers. You go to the morgue and I'll walk across."

"Are you kidding? I have to drive this contraption you call a car?"

"Okay, then you go to the restaurant and I'll go to the morgue."

"Yeah, that's better." Herman was happy now, he really didn't like my car.

I got to the morgue at 1:00 p.m. Herm came in ten minutes

later, greasy hamburgers and cold french fries in hand. Two styrofoam cups of steaming coffee were the only redeeming feature of this lunch. Just as I was about to take my first sip, Dr. Ferris came into the waiting room.

"Where's our coffee?" he asked.

"It will be right here." I told him. "Herm, give 52 Division a call quick," I whispered under my breath. "How do you take it Doctor?"

"Two medium, both black."

Sergeant Jeffery of the Identification Bureau came through the same door of the morgue and stood beside Ferris, both donning latex gloves.

"Good news Staff," he told me, "positive identification from the fingerprints."

"Great," I said, "who is she?" I got out my memo book and started writing.

"Name is Carol Lynn Millar, twenty-six years old, born in 1949."

"Okay, that's good. We need to notify the next of kin. Let's carry on with the autopsy."

Herman made two calls, one to 52 Division for the coffee, one to Sergeant Ed Valois. We had a hit. Sergeant Valois found the missing persons report on file. It had been filed on January 22, 1976 by Carol's sister-in-law and her husband when they hadn't seen her for a few days. Ed was sending a car from 14 Division to do the notification to her next of kin that she was dead.

Dr. Ferris performed the autopsy. During the examination, we found some interesting facts. The cause of death was listed as strangulation. It was also observed that the victim had received a tremendous beating before death and had actual footwear prints in her chest. The black pantyhose were removed from the right leg and examined. Another key piece of evidence, a nurse's dress was also located under the body and had been brought to the morgue. Semen stains were located on the pantyhose and the dress. It was determined that the victim had not been sexually assaulted previous to her death, however, the semen stains were more recent, meaning whoever did this crime, re-visited the body after death.

The autopsy finished, Herm and I returned to headquarters. We had a lot of work to do before we could see Douglas McCaul in the flesh and we had to get some background information that may be useful when we spoke to him in person.

Douglas Lawrence McCaul was born on September 29, 1953 in Toronto. He was one of four children, two boys and two girls. In February, 1976 he was twenty-three years old and twelve when he started stealing his sister's clothes. He set fires to cars when he was fifteen, got in trouble for auto theft, but was treated fairly lightly by the courts due to his age. When he was seventeen, he started hanging around with homosexuals and was charged with Sexual Assault after an attack on a young boy in the ravine at St. Clair Avenue and Warden. The courts looked a little more seriously at this charge and he was given two years incarceration for this crime. When he was twenty, he served time in Millbrook Detention Center. His father died the same year.

In 1975, McCaul moved to Peterborough where he lived with a minister. During the six-month period, he served time in the Peterborough jail on and off for various offences. In September 1975 he was back in Toronto and got a job at the Canadian National Railway yard located on Merton Street just east of Yonge Street. He also rented rooms in the downtown area of Toronto. His main address however, remained with his mother in the Yonge and Lawrence area, a stone's throw away from Muir Park.

We got as much detail about Douglas McCaul as we could before we paid him a visit. It was always to a Detective's advantage to have an idea about the suspect you were dealing with before confronting him; who he is, where he's been, what made him tick. Exchanging my Nash for a more professional mode of transportation that met with Herman's approval, we drove to the address listed on McCaul's identification. It was now 11:00 p.m.

We parked the unmarked Plymouth in front of the house, noting from the outside that it was well kept and situated in a quiet neighborhood. Streetlights cast a dull hue over the pathway that led to the front door. We climbed the few steps to the porch and knocked on the door. For a moment we stood in silence, listening, waiting for noises inside the house. A small porch light suddenly came on, illuminating our faces. A young man answered the door. He was with his mother.

"Are you Douglas McCaul?" I asked. I was now talking to a scrawny, nervous-looking man who I towered over and my first thought was that he could not have inflicted the injuries that I had just witnessed on the body of the deceased. His arms weren't even the size of a bamboo pole, and he was slightly hunched over making him appear even smaller. Strange looking furtive appearance.

"Yes, that's me," McCaul answered.

"I'm Staff Sergeant McCormack, Metro Toronto Police Homicide Squad. This is my partner, Sergeant Herman Lowe."

Herman stood next to me at the door.

"What's the problem officer?" McCaul's mother asked us.

"We're conducting an investigation and we'd like to speak to your son if that's okay."

McCaul appeared nervous. I saw his hands shaking. He spoke up, stepping in front of the woman. "Yeah, that's okay."

"Could we come in for a moment?" I asked.

"Sure, please come in." McCaul's mother held the door for us. She led us down a small corridor into the kitchen. He followed closely.

"What's this all about?" McCaul's mother asked.

"We think your son may have known the victim of a crime, a Miss Carol Millar."

Her face was blank. "Never heard that name." she said as she shook her head.

"Bill," Herman called. "Look at this." He was pointing at a black billfold on the table. The same type of wallet as the one we found at the murder scene. "Is this yours?" Herman asked McCaul picking it up off the table.

"Yes."

"Mind if I look at it?" Herm asked.

"No, go ahead." McCaul shrugged indifferently.

Herman turned the wallet over in his hands and found identification inside that proved it to belong to Douglas McCaul.

"Doug, we'd like you to come downtown with us. We need to ask you a few questions."

"No problem."

"Better get your stuff," Herman said, "it's cold outside."

McCaul reached for his jacket that had been hanging over the back of a chair. I noticed immediately that the knuckles on his right hand were bruised. He pulled on his boots and said, "I'm ready."

Herman took the driver's seat. I put McCaul in the back and got into the passenger seat. We made our way south to Headquarters.

"Am I under arrest?" McCaul asked in a small voice.

"No," I told him matter-of-factly. "We're investigating a Homicide."

"Wow, that's a heavy charge to lay on someone," he said

and sat back in his seat for the rest of the ride. Arriving at 590 Jarvis Street, we took him to our office on the third floor and told him that we were investigating a homicide, involving a young woman, whose body was found in Alexander Muir Park. I sat across from him, Herm stood by the door. I asked him what happened to his hand.

"Oh that, I was in a fight and I punched a newspaper box."

"When was that?" I asked him.

"I don't know, a few weeks ago. I was in a fight at the St. Clair subway station."

I took out a pad of foolscap and began to make notes. "Now Doug, I want you to know how important it is for you to tell us everything you know about this homicide."

"I'll do what I can. Can I have a smoke?" he asked, nervously tapping his fingers on the desk.

"Sure." I handed him a Winston, lit it and watched him suck back heavily on the cigarette. It was a time when everyone smoked, everywhere.

"Ready?" I asked, pen poised.

"Yeah."

"Do you work?" I began.

"Yeah, at Canadian National, Yonge and Merton."

"What have you been up to in the past couple of weeks?"

"Hanging around, working."

"Ever go downtown?"

"Yeah, I've been to a few bars downtown. The Parkside, Larry's Hideaway."

"Do you know a girl named Carol Millar?"

"Nope, never heard of her."

"So tell me. How is it that your wallet was found in the park by her body?"

"My wallet?" McCaul tried to appear shocked. "I lost my wallet. There's a report on file. if you check you'll find it."

"Lost your wallet? When and where did you lose it?" I was intrigued. Possibly, he was telling the truth.

"I left it in a cab one night. It was a Metro Cab, somewhere downtown I think. Anyway, I reported it to the police when I noticed it was gone."

"Herman, check it out."

"I'm on it." Herman picked up the phone from the vacant desk nearby. A few minutes later, he was nodding his head. "Report on file, Bill."

I asked McCaul to remove his boots. He complied. Sergeant Jeffery from the Identification Bureau came in to take photos of the boots and of McCaul's bruised hand. McCaul didn't object, as a matter of fact, he was most cooperative and insistent.

"If you don't mind Doug, I'd like to keep the boots for a while."

"Not at all. You can have them. What do you need them for?"

"I just need to check something."

"Sure you don't know Carol Millar?" I asked again.

"Nope," he responded, confidently.

"Ever been to Alexander Muir Park?"

"Years ago. I haven't been in the park in years."

"Sure about that?"

"Yup."

"Okay. That's it for tonight," and got up to leave. "Oh, would you mind if we take a sample of your spit?" I asked as an after thought.

"My spit, no I don't mind."

"Sergeant Lowe has a tissue, if you could just spit into it, we'd appreciate it. Your spit will give us your blood type and that will help eliminate you as a suspect if we find it doesn't match with our samples."

"Anything to help." McCaul smiled, taking the tissue from Herman. "Anything else?"

"I don't think so. You can go. We'll have an officer run you home."

"Thanks. If there's anything I can do, just let me know. I'll check in with you guys to see how you're making out," then he smiled as if he hadn't a care in the world.

"Good, you do that," I said, thanking him for his cooperation.

McCaul was driven home in his socks by two uniformed officers, but Herman and I weren't finished.

"What do you think?" Herm asked after McCaul left.

"I think he's lying and he thinks he has us." That was my initial impression, too.

"I'm telling you, that son of a bitch did it, I'm sure of it."

"Herm, you saw him. Do you really think he's capable? I'm sure he's involved but I don't know to what degree."

"I'm sure of it. He's lying." Herman repeated.

"If he's lying, we'll catch him. It's only a matter of time before we pick away the holes. He won't be able to stick to his story, come on, let's call it a night." It was after 2:00 a.m. "You hungry?"

"Me? Yeah, but what's open at this hour?"

"We could go down the street." There was an all night diner on the west side of Jarvis Street just south of Charles Street that we frequented. Many cases were discussed, argued, sometimes solved at that restaurant. It was a great way to unwind.

"Okay, I'm in." Herm grabbed his coat and we were out of the office quickly.

By the time we left the diner, it was after 3:00 a.m. Seven hours and we'd be back at it. When we worked a case, sleep was snatched in any increment.

Ten o'clock the next morning, we were back at Headquarters where Sergeant Jeffery from the Identification Bureau met us. Our next step was the morgue. Doctor Ferris let us have a look at the body. This time we measured the boot that we'd seized from McCaul with the imprints on the body. We had a match. The next stop we made was at the Centre of Forensic Sciences on Grosvenor Street. The boots were examined but we didn't get as lucky this time. Not a trace of blood was detected. The investigation was off to a good start with the matched boot print, but we had a lot of work to do. Over the next few days, we did much of the legwork with the help of 53 Division officers. Constable Lee Train and Peter Petruzzellis were assigned to the case.

We did verify McCaul's story about being in a fight on the subway. On Sunday January 18, 1978 at 2:12 a.m., Constable John Walker of 53 Division responded to a call at St. Clair Subway Station. It wasn't known who was the antagonist in this altercation but McCaul was indeed injured after being involved in fight. The other party was gone when the officer arrived on the scene.

We also discovered that Douglas McCaul had a problem with alcohol. He frequented the Muir Park Hotel on Yonge Street and was banned from there for his abusive and bois- terous behaviour. His sister got him into an alcohol treatment program at the Lakeshore Psychiatric Centre. It was here that he met Carol Millar, who was also a patient at the Centre. She was twenty-seven years old at the time.

Carol Millar was last seen by her relatives on Monday January 19, 1976. She left the Psychiatric Centre and arrived at her sister-in-law's house. Her sister-in-law gave her clothing, a black turtleneck sweater, underwear and checked pants but no shoes. This was the last time Carol was seen by her sister-in-law. She was reported missing three days later by her twin brother.

On Tuesday January 20, 1976, Carol Millar was seen at the Gasworks Tavern located on Yonge Street and Dundonald in the heart of downtown Toronto. The band, "Miles and Lenny," were playing and Carol Millar came into the bar at approximately 10:30 p.m. with a man. Several witnesses saw her with the man and reported that she appeared to be intoxicated. The man was loud and boisterous and threw a beer on her. At this time, Carol was still wearing the same clothing from the day before, checked pants, black turtleneck and a blue jean jacket.

Carol Millar was a small girl, missing her front teeth which made her distinctive. She had short dark hair. She was seen leaving the bar with the same man some time later. This is the last time anyone saw Carol Millar alive. Later that night, a witness reported to police that she had heard a female screaming in Muir Park.

During this period of investigation, I would get calls from McCaul, asking how the case was going and if we had any leads. I asked him if he'd ever been to the Gasworks Tavern. He told me that he had never been there.

On February 12, 1976, we once again spoke to the suspect and I brought him into the office. He gave me a much more detailed statement about his actions over the past two months but his story was full of holes. This time, we decided to look further into the loss of his wallet. He stated that on Saturday January 24, 1976 at approximately 6:00 a.m., he got a ride from 32 Division officers, Police Constable Bruce Keay and Constable John Clarke. They picked him up at Yonge and Deloraine where he was running to catch a bus and gave him a drive to Yonge and Lawrence. McCaul stated that he did not get on a bus but instead got into a taxi that took him to work at Yonge and Merton Street and it was in this cab that he lost his wallet.

. Later, I found out a completely different story. After speaking to the officers, I discovered that Constable Keay and Constable Clarke did in fact pick McCaul up and drove him to Yonge and Lawrence. This was where the story changed. They watched him get onto a southbound bus. Further, fellow employees from the CN yard told us that McCaul did not show up to work at all this date. He was lying to us and we were on to him. Constable Clarke then came into the office while McCaul was giving me this story and he positively identified McCaul as being the man he gave a ride to.

Although McCaul did report the wallet lost, there were inconsistencies with his story. He went into 53 Division on Monday January 26, 1976 at 2:00 p.m. in the afternoon and reported it to Cadet James Dunn. First glance at the report backs his story up, until we interviewed the cadet himself. McCaul told the cadet that he lost the wallet on January 24th and asked him to backdate the report to the time of the murder. Sure that he now had an ironclad alibi for the wallet, he left the police station.

Throughout this investigation, we utilized several officers from different units. 53 Division was used as a temporary office for us to conduct our business. Sergeant Don Madigan and Sergeant Patrick O'Brien from the General Assignment Squad were attached to the case. These officers would do much of the investigative and leg work for us. It was through their efforts and the other officers assigned, that we received much of the evidence and the background we needed to lay the Charge.

Constables Lee Train and Peter Petruzzellis investigated several witnesses. Three of whom could identify McCaul and the victim and place them in the Gasworks Tavern together on the night of the murder. It was decided that we would conduct a "line-up" with these witnesses for the purpose of identification. On Tuesday February 17, 1976, Constable Train arranged to take McCaul to the Bloor and Yonge Subway Station and mingle him amongst the people there. The three witnesses were brought into the station where one of them picked McCaul out as being the man with Carol Millar at the Gasworks. Constable Train then returned with McCaul to my office and advised me of the results. McCaul took a seat in front of my desk.

"Doug," I started, "I want to read a caution to you."

"Go ahead." He tried to appear uninterested.

"Okay, I am advising you that you may be charged with the offence of Homicide. You are not obliged to say anything unless you wish to do so but whatever you say may be given in evidence against you. Do you understand?"

"Yeah." His hands were folded in his lap and he stared at them, refusing to meet my eyes, he was restless, constantly changing position in the wooden chair. He sure didn't appear as confident as he did the first time we met him.

"The witnesses today have made a positive identification of you," I informed him matter-of-factly, "they told us that you were for sure the guy they had seen with Carol Millar at the Gasworks Tavern on January 20, 1976."

"It's a lie, they are lying!" His head snapped up, lips quivering.

"Do you think so, Doug?" I asked calmly.

"Yes. They're all lying. I may have been mistaken about my wallet, I'm not sure. I want to speak to my lawyer." He sat back down in the chair, shoulders slumped.

"Okay, I'll call him for you." I picked up the receiver and dialed the number. McCaul was represented by Mr. Barry McKague. Barry had a law practice with his cousin John

Carriere. It was John Carriere who answered the phone. Barry was not in, but John advised that he would be right down. We waited for him to arrive.

"I know I've made a few mistakes in what I told you." McCaul had regained control of himself. "There's a few mistakes about bars, about the cab. I know I lost my wallet." He started to cry.

"Why are you crying?" I asked him. "Herm, can you get him a tissue?"

Herman shot me a look, he didn't like the guy and wasn't buying the tears. He then noticed the box our secretary Sandra Morgan had on her desk. Walking over to the desk, he took out one single sheet and handed it to McCaul.

"Thank you." McCaul took the tissue and wiped his eyes. "They are all mistaken," he continued. "I'm innocent. I never hurt anyone, any girl, anybody. I'm innocent!"

He kept up the tears, although much slower now, every now and again lifting his head to see if we were watching. John Carriere arrived at the office and asked to speak to McCaul alone. Herman and I left the room, allowing them privacy. When Carriere was finished, he asked us a few questions with a much more subdued McCaul beside him. We answered the questions to his satisfaction. Once again, McCaul was let go.

The next piece of information came from one of McCaul's friends. He reported that McCaul had visited him on the day the body was found in the park. McCaul told his friend about the police finding the body. He gave him several details about the condition, position and shape of the body. Much of this information had not been released to the press or the public. We were forming a tighter web around our boy and he didn't seem to notice, we worked on the case day and night with the assistance of many police officers that had been assigned to investigate different avenues. Some investigated McCaul's past, others spoke to witnesses and many used their expertise to analyze every scrap of evidence that had been collected at the scene.

In the meantime, McCaul had work of his own to do. He went back to Peterborough for a visit. On Saturday, February 21, 1976, he was hitting the bottle heavily, attending various downtown Peterborough hotels. After leaving one of the establishments, he was involved in an assault where he was the victim. Constable Gordon of the Peterborough Police was patrolling at about 11:00 p.m. when a citizen alerted him to an altercation taking place on a street corner. When Constable Gordon arrived, he found Douglas McCaul lying on the pavement, bleeding profusely. Constable Gordon took him to the Peterborough hospital where he was treated and later released and the next day, returned home to Toronto.

The facts were mounting. On Wednesday, February 25, 1976, after a few days of mild weather, Emergency Task Force officers once again searched the area of the murder. Constable Andrews got lucky and located a gray dress close to the scene, it appeared to be a nurse's uniform. He turned it over to us. This was the second nurse's uniform found at the scene. McCaul's sister positively identified both dresses as belonging to her. We knew that Carol Millar had nothing to do with the medical profession and it was now obvious that McCaul had returned to the scene of the murder on a few occasions and tried to dress the body in this attire. Time was ripe to close our net and close it quickly.

The next day, Thursday, February 26, 1976 at 6:00 p.m., we had all our ducks in a row, all the evidence to lay a murder charge. I instructed Sergeant Don Madigan and Sergeant Patrick O'Brien to make the arrest. They attended McCaul's address and arrested him. McCaul was waiting for them.

"Douglas McCaul?" Don Madigan was met by a young

man who had opened the front door. Don knew it was McCaul because he had been doing much of the investigative work, talking to witnesses and showing them McCaul's picture.

"Yeah?"

"I am Sergeant Madigan, this is my partner, Sergeant O'Brien. You're under arrest on a charge of murder."

"Oh my God!" McCaul exclaimed, partially hiding himself behind the oak door.

"Do you mind if we step in?" O'Brien stuck his foot inside the opening, anticipating the door being suddenly closed.

McCaul opened the door, allowing the officers to step inside the foyer.

"Do you understand what we just told you?" Madigan asked. McCaul nodded.

"Okay, I will now read you the caution. You have the right to retain and instruct counsel without delay, further, do you wish to say anything in answer to the charge? You are not obliged to say anything but be advised that anything you do say may be given in evidence. Do you understand?"

"Yeah, I knew you guys were coming, I'm innocent partly." McCaul relented.

Sergeant Madigan and Sergeant O'Brien then drove McCaul to police headquarters. They were all taken aback when they drove into the rear parking lot where a slew of reporters, cameras, microphones were waiting for them. It was uncertain how the media got wind of this one, someone had alerted them, no doubt someone from within.

"Oh Christ, it's the press! Can I cover my head?" McCaul asked, glancing out the side window of the car.

He was allowed to pull his tweed jacket over his head, somewhat hiding his face from the media. Lights flashed and microphones were thrust forward effectively blocking their way to the rear entrance. It would be a few tense moments before they got him out of the car and into the building. Once inside, the trio took the elevator to the third floor. Herman and I were waiting in the office. Sergeant Madigan handed McCaul over to me.

"Doug, you know why you're here?" I asked.

"Yeah, they told me," he shrugged.

Douglas McCaul was formerly charged with the offence of Non Capital Murder. He was taken from headquarters to the Don Jail and served what police call "dead time" until his trial could be held. The trial was held in December that same year before Supreme Court Justice Mr. Hughes and a twelve person jury. Mr. Robert Magee was the Crown Attorney assigned to the case. Several witnesses took the stand as well as three Doctors of Psychiatry. The trial concluded on the ninth of December, 1976 with a finding of "Not Guilty by Reason of Insanity." He was a psychopath and had black outs due to alcohol which both contributed to these findings. Douglas McCaul was then sent to Penetanguishene Psychiatric Hospital on a Lieutenant Governor's warrant. The case was closed, or so the police thought.

McCaul's lawyer, Barry McKague and I became friends until his untimely death from a heart attack in 1995. In the fall of 1977, almost a year after the case against McCaul was concluded, Barry gave me a call. McCaul wanted to talk to us. He had some information about another murder. All he wanted in return was immunity. I arrived at work on a crisp morning in November, ready to see Douglas McCaul again.

"Herm, up for a little ride today?" I asked my partner as I walked through the door of the office. He was already there, coffee mug in one hand, pen in the other.

"Sure, where we going?" He was curious, probably wondering what jalopy I would make him ride in this time.

"North. Penetanguishene."

His eyebrows formed a tight weave across his forehead. "Penetanguishene! Why are we going there?"

"We're going to visit an old friend."

"Okay, I'll bite. An old friend? Who?"

"Douglas McCaul." I smiled.

Herman lifted a single eyebrow. "Douglas McCaul?"

"That's right, you heard me." I sat down in the chair opposite his desk.

"I thought we were finished with him."

"So did I. Apparently he wants to talk."

"Okay, I'll go with you, but I'm not getting into that circus toy you call a car."

I laughed, knowing that's what was really bothering him. "Don't worry, we'll take a police car, it's official business."

Herm smiled and was ready as I got my things together, picked up a set of car keys and headed for the door. Penetanguishene is about a two-hour drive north and west of Toronto. It's a small community with many of its residents employed by the psychiatric hospital.

As soon as we arrived, we were ushered into a private room containing two chairs and a couch. In a matter of minutes, McCaul was brought to the door.

"Hi Doug," I greeted as he stepped into the room. He hadn't changed much and seemed quite content in his new home, but still, the skinny, disheveled man I remembered from the previous year.

"Staff Sergeant McCormack, did you have to bring him with you?" McCaul frowned, motioning to Herman with his thumb, his dislike of Herm all too evident.

"Yeah, he's my partner. There has to be two of us." Herman tried to hold back a smile.

"Okay then. If that's how it has to be." McCaul resigned

himself to the fact that there would be two of us conducting the interview. He focused on me, taking a seat on the couch.

Herman and I each chose a chair. I brought out a pad of foolscap and got ready to write. "What do you want to tell us Doug?" I asked.

"Can I have a smoke?"

"Sure." Pulling the package of cigarettes from my breast pocket, I tapped one out. He took it between tar-stained fingers and lifted it to his lips and I lit it for him.

McCaul sucked back deeply, holding the cigarette tight between his fingers as if it were his last. "I was told by my lawyer that I might not get charged if I talked to you guys," he said.

"That depends on what you have to say. I can't tell you we won't charge you, that's a decision the Attorney General will have to make. Still want to talk?"

"Yeah I do. I trust you. I'm ready to talk."

I read him the standard caution. He stated he understood. Herman and I sat back while McCaul went on to tell us about a murder he'd committed in 1971 when he was eighteen.

* * *

On June 10 1971, Douglas McCaul was drinking at the Jolly Miller Tavern located on the east side of Yonge Street north of Lawrence Avenue. Archibald MacDougall was also drinking there that night. Archie was a frequent patron of the tavern and was there on this occasion with his two nephews. He was sixty-two years old, the caretaker for the Loretto Abbey Private School for Girls. When Archie left the bar at the end of the night, his nephews thought he left alone. He was, in fact, with Douglas McCaul.

It was a quiet night out on Yonge Street, not much in the

way of vehicular or pedestrian traffic. They decided to take a short cut through a park across the street, the same park that Archie's nephews said he was afraid to walk in alone. It was late, but it was a bright warm June night and there were two of them. Archie MacDougall was well liked, often buying rounds for the customers of the bar. He lived on the Loretto Abbey School grounds and often followed the pathway through the park to his residence. He usually did this alone and only in the daytime. That was not to be this night. As soon as they were out of sight of the street, Douglas McCaul brought out a small paring knife. Wielding the knife wildly, he stabbed the older man several times until he lay still on the ground.

Not content, McCaul further used the knife on Archie's face, mutilating it as best he could. McCaul went through the pockets of the dead man but there was nothing worth taking but a pocketful of change.

Taking off on foot, McCaul left the victim's cigarette lighter, comb and handkerchief behind. There were no witnesses. A nun from the Loretto Abbey found the body the next day and she called the police immediately. McCaul was never apprehended and even admitted returning to the scene the following day when news of the body being found was released. He watched with the other spectators as the police contained the scene. He had not even been a suspect, until now. He told us that he'd been receiving treatment since he'd been in the hospital and was remembering some things he'd previously forgotten due to the blackouts that were brought on by drinking. The facts he remembered about the MacDougall case implicated him explicitly. He was the killer.

Herman and I confirmed his story with the investigating officers of the MacDougall case, Staff Sergeant Weatherbie and Sergeant Read. In every case, there are details held back from the media, intimate information that is not released. In this case, the facts about the mutilation of the victim were not released. McCaul made reference to this and provided us with an exact description. Douglas McCaul had detailed knowledge of this homicide and reiterated facts only the killer knew. Herman and I left the hospital, statement in hand.

"What do you think?" I asked Herm on the ride home.

"Oh, he did it all right, makes me wonder what else that boy's been up to."

"Me too. Do you think the charge will fly?"

Herman lit up a smoke, exhaling out the partially open window. "Do you?"

"No. I'd be surprised if we get a chance to lay this one on him."

I was right. We took the statement to the Attorney General. It was decided that McCaul would not be prosecuted in relation to this offence as he was certified to be within Section Sixteen of the Criminal Code of Canada that confirmed he was legally insane and would only be found not guilty by reason of insanity once again if we charged him. The case was marked solved. No charges laid."

* * *

That was the last Dad had heard of Douglas McCaul until he was charged again in 1987 with Attempted Murder and I made my call to him that morning. McCaul served only five years in Penetanguishene before he was transferred to St. Thomas where he was on the prowl again. As of today, Douglas McCaul remains a resident of Penetanguishene Psychiatric Hospital. The third murder he bragged about to the cab driver to this date remains unsolved.

APR 4 1987 SUN
APR 4 1987 SUN

Freed insane killer now held in knifing

By (Dord) MacDougall, Archie

Our hands are tied

The *Sun* cannot name the man in Mark Bono-koski's column on this page.

To do so, we would be breaking the law — it's called contempt of court.

The law says we can't publish a man's criminal past once he has been charged with a new crime. Why this man is afforded such protection, on top of the incredible freedom he has already been given, is beyond us.

The judicial system in this case should not only be strengthened but perhaps changed. Halton Police Chief James Harding is frustrated about laws that seem to protect criminals more than victims, and rightly so.

You read Bono's column and tell us what you think.

Call us with your views and we'll publish some of them in tomorrow's Sunday *Sun*.

Ring our switchboard at 947-2222 today between noon and 2:30 p.m. only and have your say.

Maybe we can make our lawmakers listen.

Les Pyette, Sun Executive Editor.

MARK BONOKOSKI

E leven years ago he was ruled insane in a murder so brutal and sordid that the judge refused to allow the press to print details — yet he has been loose, almost full time, since last October.

His release, and subsequent arrest on an attempted murder charge in Burlington, has so outraged the Halton Regional Police chief that he has issued a challenge to the media to present the facts concerning a situation he calls a "symphony of dangerous stupidity."

Six days ago, at 1:18 a.m., Metro Police Constables Kevin Demoe and Steven Harrigan, of 53 Division, spotted a wanted red-and-white motor scooter on Erskine Ave. and arrested a man for the attempted murder the day before in an ungrooked knife attack on a Burlington woman in the Super Centre parking lot.

After a brief foot chase through a parkette, the man was taken into custody, along with a bag of women's clothing he was prone to wearing in private moments.

Charged was a 33-year-old closet transvestite, the same person the public mistakenly believed was still locked away in a hospital for the criminally insane, which is what the Penetang Mental Health Centre was called when he was admitted in December 1976.

Sources have now indicated he is also under investigation for similar attacks the same day on two other women — one in the town of Dundas and another in the Mississauga area.

There are 400 in-patients and 2,000 out-patients at the St. Thomas Psychiatric Hospital, and it was there that this man was transferred. But the hospital would not say when the man was actually moved out of Penetang. Nor would it confirm any details.

"Confidentiality requirements as outlined by the Mental Health Act does not allow me to comment on anything regarding any patient," said hospital spokesman William Lewis. "The law prohibits me 100%."

Police sources in Halton region, however, have indicated that he arrived at St. Thomas from the maximum-security asylum in Penetang in 1981 and was granted a full-time pass from the hospital in October 1986. The proviso for his freedom were that he maintain full-time employment, that he reside at a St. Thomas boarding house on Chester St. and that he report to the hospital on certain specified days.

Those, apparently, were his only shackles.

On March 19, however, and for reasons unstated, the hospital yanked in the man's rope, demanding he return to the hospital each day after his job was done.

When he failed to return six days ago, a warrant was struck and a Telex message to arrest on sight went out to all police forces in Ontario.

Yesterday, Halton Police Chief James Harding, whose force patrols Burlington, issued this statement:

forgiving, and intellectually understanding of those who choose to commit even the most heinous of crimes," said Harding's written release. "They probably took great pride in the fact that they had a hand in delivering freedom to such as those.

"They are the same people who will hide behind a jungle of philosophical jargon and develop all manner of reasons to justify those convicted of serious crimes against a person walking the streets.

"I suggest you take their intellectuality and reasons to the victims that have been, are now, and will eventually be, and try to convince them to understand and support concepts that put the well-being of the criminal before the safety of the victim and potential victim.

"I challenge you, and your newspaper, or any other newspaper or agency for that matter, to use the horror of this latest incident to make the slightest bit of difference to this cretonic situation.

"During the last decade, if incidents such as this were to be counted as musical notes, we could write a symphony of dangerous stupidity.

"The sad thing is, no one will listen."

The man's journey to official insanity began on Feb. 8, 1976, when a citizen walking his dog through Alexander Muir Park stumbled upon a compost heap and the frozen body of 25-year-old Carol Lynn Millar.

The facts of the case were so grisly that Ontario Supreme Court Justice Samuel Hughes barred the public and the press from the courtroom "in the interest of public morals" — with no further elaboration.

The night before she disappeared, Millar failed to return to the Lakeshore Psychiatric Hospital, where she was undergoing alcoholism treatment. He was seen in the Gasworks Tavern on Yonge St. with a greasy-looking character later confirmed to be the suspect.

And that was the last time she was seen — until the snow began to thaw three weeks later and a badly-beaten and semi-naked body began to emerge from a bin of decomposing vegetation.

Now, 11 years later, Millar's brother, a 39-year-old roofer named Roland Millar, is left wondering who is standing guard to protect the public.

"I cannot believe this man is already out," he said. "Who are these people and how can they justify his release? Let's face it, this man is not cured."

Deputy Chief William McCormack was in the homicide squad then, teamed with his long-time partner, Herman Lowe, who died two weeks ago of cancer.

HALTON POLICE CHIEF JAMES HARDING: "A symphony of dangerous stupidity."

To McCormack, the man he charged with Millar's murder was "one of the strangest characters I'd come across in a long time. That guy is really, really weird (and) really, really dangerous.

When the suspect finally went to trial for that murder, he was found not guilty by reason of insanity. Most of his brain damage apparently came from acute alcoholism, so acute he would suffer blackouts when he lingered for days at a time.

What the public never got to know was that McCormack and Lowe were able to close the books on another murder that occurred five years before Millar was so savagely killed.

In that case, Archie MacDougall, a 62-year-old caretaker for the Loretto Abbey private school for girls, was found stabbed to death on June 19, 1971, in a park across from the Jolly Miller Tavern on Yonge St.

His pockets were turned inside-out and his face had been mutilated with the point of a paring knife.

"We approached the attorney general's department about laying murder charges against (the man) on that one," said McCormack, "but since he had just been ruled insane in the Millar case, it was thought the outcome would be the same on this one.

"But at least the file could be marked solved."

W hen the accused went off to Penetang on a lieutenant-governor's warrant, his term was indefinite. But, as early as six months after he was committed, he received his first review by the five-person panel that oversees the release of psychiatric inmates — and every year which followed.

Chaired by a supreme court judge, the panel has two psychiatrists, a lawyer, and a layman.

A former member of that panel last week described the reviews as being "a quest of prediction. You know 80% of those released will never be a problem. It's just a matter of predicting the correct 80%."

To McCormack, however, the man's history should have negated any release.

"There was never any doubt in my mind that he was, to put it bluntly, a nut if there ever was a nut," said McCor-

POLICE

Manslaughter

"The unlawful killing of a
human being without
malicious intent."

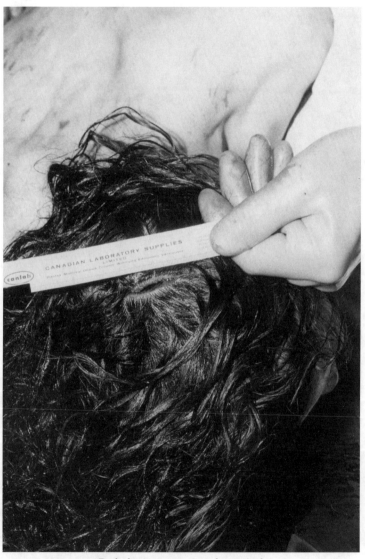

Pathologist measuring the wound
on the back of a deceased female's head.

CHAPTER TWO

EDWARD JAMES TOLAN

THE YEAR WAS 1972 and it had not started well. Three Toronto Police Officers would lose their lives that year, killed in the line of duty in the first trimester of the year. Detective Mike Irwin, Detective Doug Sinclair and Constable Donald Lewis. Three young, talented police officers, snatched away in the prime of their lives. Constable Lewis was killed in a motor vehicle accident on February 11, 1972. Mike Irwin and Doug Sinclair would meet their fate two weeks later.

The murder toll in Toronto continued on an even scale in 1972. Notably, the majority of victims in the seventies and eighties were largely women and most, taken violently by a partner or spouse. A statistic that unfortunately hasn't changed much in the past three decades.

* * *

I n 1972, I was twelve. Perfectly content in my world of safety, school and home, completely oblivious to murder. Instead, I was focusing my thoughts and fears on the new school I was attending after my family had moved from the "upper beaches" area of Toronto to the Scarborough Bluff area. I had great dreams for the future, one that included writing fiction, becoming wealthy and spending my days on the sunny shores of a faraway exotic island. It was during that summer that my father and I were out for a drive, headed for a downtown Toronto dry cleaners, that I first had an inkling that perhaps, I might be suited for investigative work.

Seated in the passenger seat of the 1963 Buick Wildcat, I glanced to my right and noticed the car stopped at the traffic light beside us. There was one man driving and another male passenger. Something about them didn't look right. I couldn't put my finger on it but I knew they were up to something.

"Look at these guys Dad, they don't look right to me," I said.

"I've been watching them for some time," Dad replied without taking his eyes from the road. "Saw them a while back. I know those two guys, I've arrested the driver before for break and enter. Reach into the glove box, there's a pencil and a pad in there. Write down the license plate number for me. Could you do that?"

"Sure." The light turned green and both cars went on their way again. I scribbled the numbers down and tore the page off, handing it to him. He took the paper, folded it and shoved it into his top pocket. We rode the rest of the way to the cleaners in silence.

Later that week, he arrived home from work with something important to tell me.

"Remember those two guys in the car beside us the other day, the one where you wrote down the license plate?"

"Yeah, I remember," I answered eagerly.

"They were arrested today for a break and enter that they did in that area right before we saw them. We matched the plate with what a witness saw and bingo, it was them!"

"Hey, that's great Dad." I was so proud. I recognized two criminals without any one else's assistance.

"Yeah, good work Kiddo!" Dad walked into the kitchen and kissed my mom. "What's for dinner?"

* * *

Tuesday August 15, 1972 started out to be a warm humid night in the city of Toronto. The family was fast asleep in our non air-conditioned home that we shared atop the Scarborough Bluffs. Screened in windows allowed a tease of the summer night's breeze to sweep through the bedrooms.

It was about 4:00 a.m. when the sound of the phone ringing woke my dad. The upstairs phone had been moved to his side of the bed since he transferred to the Homicide Squad.

"Hello," I heard my dad cough into the phone, not conscious of time or day for that matter. "Okay, I'm on my way." He hung up the receiver. "Got to go," he whispered to my mom. "Got a homicide."

"Be careful," she warned him, rolling over to the warmth on his side of the bed before shutting her eyes again.

"I will," he assured.

At the time of her death on August 15, 1972, Ann Price was thirty-five years old and had been in and out of an abusive relationship with Edward Tolan for the last year. From the first day the two had met, it was a stormy relationship. They moved in together, had fights where Ann left and Edward demanded she return, under the threat of death or bodily harm. Ann always came back – due mostly to fear.

Ann Price met Edward Tolan in the downtown area of

Toronto where she frequently hung out with friends. Ann was unemployed, had serious drug problems and Edward had recently come to Toronto after a string of encounters with the law in his hometown of Brantford, Ontario. He wanted to make a clean sweep of it after just being released from Kingston Penitentiary, Canada's oldest and meanest maximum security prison.

Theirs was a doomed relationship from the start. Ann was sick, mostly from the years of drug and alcohol abuse. She was often in trouble with the police for minor thefts and drugs and rarely kept the same address. Ann was a tiny woman with a slight, frail figure. She was less than half the size of Edward Tolan. Armed with a previous history of abuse and assault, Edward brought his aggressive, forceful qualities to his new relationship.

Edward Tolan was born in Brantford, Ontario and started his criminal career there when he was sixteen years old. He traded in his schooling for truck driving when he wasn't in jail. By the time he was thirty-three, he was not only a career criminal, but also an alcoholic. Edward mostly got himself in trouble by stealing cars, committing frauds and assaulting people. The longest sentence he ever received was for a period of two years, of which he served eighteen months, until June 14, 1966 when he committed the first crime that would put him away for more than just a few months. Manslaughter.

It was a warm afternoon in the summer of 1966 when Edward Tolan decided to visit a friend who rented a room on the main floor of the rooming house next door. Albert Dungey was twenty-nine years old and was happy to have the company, someone else to drink with. Edward brought with him his 12-gauge shotgun, to show his friend. After a period of time, a loud bang was heard throughout the house and Albert Dungey had a belly full of buckshot. Several occupants of the rooming house ran to the main floor hallway where they saw Albert, propped up against a door, bleeding profusely from the left side of his body.

Albert was transported to the Brantford General Hospital where he underwent surgery for his injuries. He died at 1:15a.m. on the morning of June 16, 1966. Edward remained at the scene of the shooting until the police arrived. He was adamant that it had been an accident. He didn't know the gun was loaded. After receiving word from the hospital that Albert died, Sergeant of Detectives, Crocock and Constable James Farnworth of the Brantford Police charged Edward Tolan with Manslaughter. On September 26, 1966, Edward pleaded guilty to the offence and was sentenced to six years in Kingston Penitentiary. He did not serve his full sentence and was out on parole by September 16, 1970. Within two months of his release, he was right back on track and without missing a beat, he quickly resumed his career of assaults and weapon offences. It was early 1971 when he met Ann Price, another casualty in his long line of conquests.

Because of Ann Price's small physical stature, she was an easy target for the much stronger Tolan. Edward Tolan was the icing on the cake. In the year she spent with him, he would repeat his cycle of violence followed by affection. Her only reprieve came when he was sentenced to serve jail time for the petty crimes he was committing during their troubled time together.

It was during one of these periods of incarceration in the Don Jail, during the month of August 1972 that Ann met Scott Anderson at Norm's Grill in downtown Toronto. Ann frequented the restaurant and often sat with Scott, an unemployed laborer who had become crippled in an industrial accident. It was evident to Scott that Ann had no place to stay so he offered his apartment. During the second week of August, she took him up on his offer and moved in.

On Saturday, August 12, 1972, Scott and Ann went out for a bite to eat at a Greek restaurant downtown. A friend of Ann's came up to the table to tell her that Edward Tolan had been released from the Don Jail and he was looking for her. Flustered, Ann gave her friend the phone number where she was residing.

"Tell Edward to call me at this number," she said, hurriedly placing the number in his hand. Ann and Scott left the restaurant and headed back to the apartment. They were home for ten minutes when the phone started to ring. It was Edward. He demanded to know where she was. Ann gave him the address.

At about 8:00 p.m., Edward Tolan showed up at the apartment and Scott let him in.

"Ann's sleeping," he told Edward. "She isn't feeling too good."

"I want to see her." Edward said, making his way toward the bedroom. He entered the room, closing the door behind him. A few hours later, Edward and Ann came into the living room. Scott left them there and went to bed.

The next morning, August 13th, Scott woke up around 10:00 a.m. Edward and Ann were still in the living room and appeared to be in good spirits. Scott went out for the day, returning at dinnertime. Edward was sleeping on the couch and Ann in the armchair so he went to bed.

The next morning when Scott awoke, Edward was still there. He and Ann hadn't left the place in two days. Scott decided to go out again, not wanting to interfere in the couple's privacy and returned around 7:00 p.m., bringing a bottle of wine with him. Ann had dinner ready and the three of them ate and had a couple of glasses of wine. After dinner,

Scott had to go out. A couple of his friends owed him some money and he needed to collect it. He picked up a friend and headed downtown then returned home around 11:30 p.m. Ann and Edward were again in the living room only this time, the situation was not so amicable.

Scott went into the kitchen and sat down at the table. Ann followed, pulling out the chair across from Scott's and sat down. Edward appeared at the doorway.

"Why don't you tell me the truth? What are you covering up?" Edward challenged.

Ann shook her head. She'd been through this before, jealous fits, false accusations. She remained silent, refusing to answer.

Her silence infuriated Edward. Abruptly, he grabbed Ann by the sweater, pulling her out of the chair, slamming her against the kitchen cabinet. She slid to the floor, groaning in pain.

"You're a whore, nothing but a whore." Edward was working himself into a frenzy. He kicked Ann repeatedly. Her head started to bleed.

"Stop it Edward!" Scott yelled, coming slowly to his feet.

"Sit down and stay out of his. I'm going to kill her before the night is through, then I'm going to kill you!" Edward screamed. Scott was mortified, helpless due to his condition, he backed into the living room toward the phone.

"Don't touch that phone," Edward warned. Scott was scared. He did what he was told. Edward bent down and picked Ann's limp body up. He carried her into the bedroom and laid her on the bed.

"Tell me the truth Ann, answer me," Edward repeated twice.

There was no response. Edward left the room, picked up the phone and made a call. Scott wasn't sure who he was talking to, but he was getting increasingly angrier. Slamming down the receiver, Edward went back into the bedroom and lifted Ann, throwing her down on the cold tiles of the front hallway.

"Tell the truth Ann, tell the truth!" He screamed at her now still form. When she didn't answer, he picked her up again and threw her into the living room where she dropped to the floor. Edward was crazed, kicking her all over her body, again and again.

"Stop it!" Scott yelled.

"You shut up or I'll kill you for sure! I don't give a fuck about her, I've got nothing to lose. Nobody else is going to have her by the time I'm finished with her. I'm going to the Pen, I have nothing to lose!"

"She used me for a sucker," Edward complained loudly. Scott looked at Ann who hadn't moved. Edward picked her up again, carrying her back into the bedroom where he laid her on the bed.

"Scott, come in here!" he yelled.

Scott went into the room.

"She's not breathing, her lips are black." Edward looked scared. He had finally gone too far.

"I'm calling an ambulance," Scott said.

"Yeah, maybe you better." Edward agreed, calming.

The ambulance arrived with the fire department and found Ann with vital signs absent. They rushed her to the hospital, making a valiant attempt to resuscitate her. The police arrived at the apartment shortly after but found that Edward had already left with Scott and was on his way to St. Joseph's Hospital. When the officers arrived at the emergency department, they were told that Ann was dead and it looked suspicious.

Police Constable Keith Cowling arrived at the hospital in

time to hear that Ann Price had been pronounced dead. Edward Tolan was there.

"I don't believe she's dead, she can't be dead," he said to the officer.

"I'm truly sorry for your loss," Constable Cowling told him, not exactly sure of what had transpired. "Is there anything I can do?"

"Fuck off, I'm going for a walk," Edward responded, dismissing the officer.

"I'm afraid you'll have to stay here, sir." Cowling told Edward. Scott sat glumly in the Emergency waiting room.

"Fuck you all, I didn't kill her, I'm going to find out who did. Someone at the fucking Norm's Grill! You won't have to bother me with that place after I've finished."

Sergeant Fowler and Detectives Greer and Korchuk from 14 Division arrived at the hospital as he was finishing his speech.

After identifying themselves, Detective Greer told him, "Mr. Tolan, you'll have to come with us."

Edward agreed and went quietly with the detectives. At 14 Division, the officers sat him in an interview room. Constable Cowling remained with him.

"It's a real bummer that's she's dead, you know?" Edward told the officer.

"Yes it is," Cowling answered.

"It's my fault. I went out to get a bottle of wine and when I came back, she was lying on the floor in the living room. She spoke to me saying, 'Get me on the bed Eddy'."

Cowling could see that Tolan was building his alibi.

"Yeah, that's what she said so I lifted her up and she wasn't bleeding until I got on the bed and then I thought she was having a seizure and started to give her mouth to mouth when all of a sudden, blood came out of her nose. I don't really believe she's dead. I suppose I'm number one suspect. I can't really prove I didn't do anything, and she had a black eye when I saw her at the hospital."

"You'll have to tell your side of it to the detectives." Cowling told him, but Edward continued.

"I really don't give a fuck now. She was all I had. I really loved her even though nobody else thought so. Do you think she could have had a seizure?"

"I don't know," Cowling replied.

"What will happen now?" Edward asked.

"I couldn't tell you, the detectives will be in to talk to you in a minute," Cowling told him.

"You know, lots of times I lost my head. We were both going to get out of Toronto. I thought she was straightening out. I was the last one to see her so I suppose, I'm number one suspect. I tell you, I was sitting on the couch with Ann and we had a big jug of wine. I went out to get some more and when I came back, she was lying on the floor by the couch. I took her into the bedroom and all this blood came down her nose and I started to give her mouth to mouth and told Scott to call the police. I didn't know where she got that black eye. She was sick you know, she fell out of a car a while back and that's why she had a couple of cuts on her head."

Cowling got up. "Like a smoke?" he asked.

"Yeah." Edward took the cigarette from the officer. "I should have stayed home. Anybody could have come in there while I was gone and done this to her and now I just walked right in the fucking place like an idiot. What a position to be in." He shook his head.

Detective Walter Korchuk of 14 Division had been busy covering the bases and interviewing the witnesses. He was armed with a good deal of facts from Scott Anderson and the doctors at St. Joseph's Hospital before he went back to the office.

"Call the Homicide Squad," Korchuk told Detective Bert Novis as he walked through the door of the busy second floor detective office at 14 Division. "Where is he?" Korchuk asked, referring to their number one suspect.

"In there." Novis indicated the interview room at the back of the office.

Detective Novis set down the phone. "Homicide's on the way," he told Korchuk.

Just then, Edward Tolan opened the door to the outer office. "I'm not staying in this fucking room, I want to stay in the big room!" he yelled.

"You have to stay in there for now," Novis instructed.

Tolan didn't like the answer and started through the door.

"You fucking cops are trying to pin a murder rap on me. You prick, I'll kill all the bastards at Norm's Grill. I didn't kill her." He started to cry. "I didn't punch her, she got hit by a car two weeks ago. She kept picking her head, it kept bleeding. I just found her lying there."

Novis took him back to the room where he again read the standard caution to Tolan. "Do you understand this?" Novis asked when he had finished reading.

"Fuck off," Edward responded.

"Who's your lawyer?" Novis asked.

"Fuck off, I'm not telling you anything."

"That's your prerogative." Novis agreed. "Now get back into that room."

"You're not big enough to keep me in this fucking room." Edward stated. What he didn't realize was Bert Novis was indeed big enough to keep him in that room. Edward decided to try his luck, punching the bigger officer in the jaw. The punch slid off the lower part of Detective Novis's face.

"Finished?" Novis asked, smiling.

Edward Tolan looked up. Wrong guy to mess with. "Yup, finished," he answered and went back into the room.

This is where my dad picks up the case.

* * *

I had been in the Homicide Squad for three years by 1972 and George Thompson was my regular partner. On August 15th, 1972, he was on holidays and I was on call. It never failed, get into a great sleep after a long day and without a doubt, the shrill ringing of that telephone would be enough to shatter any hope of recapturing that blessed feeling.

This was to be the case on August 15th when the calm of my slumber was broken by that noise at 4:00 a.m. 14 Division were investigating an apparent murder and they were requesting our attendance.

Within the hour, I had showered, shaved, dressed in a clean suit and arrived at 590 Jarvis Street, making my way to the third floor office. I was met there by Detective Bill Kerr. Bill's regular partner was off on holidays as well, so it would be him I teamed up with for this one. Bill and I would once again team up years later when I became the Chief of Police and Bill was one of my deputies.

At 5:25 a.m., coffee in hand, we left headquarters and made our way to 14 Division, one of the oldest of Toronto's police stations located off Dundas Street, west of Bathurst. Once there, we spoke to Detective Bert Novis who advised us that the suspect was being held in the interview room. He gave us the location for the offence and Bill and I decided to go there first. When we arrived at 1577 Dundas Street West, we immediately went to the third floor apartment and met Police Constable Stephen Mugford who was standing guard at the door. He allowed us in after jotting our names, rank and badge numbers in his memo book.

Detective John Christie of the Identification Bureau had already arrived and was busy snapping photos. Detective Korchuk and Detective Greer were in the hallway of the apartment. Sergeant Fowler had just taken the statement from Scott Anderson and the detectives handed it to me to read over. Bill Kerr and I immediately began taking detailed notes in our memo books. It would be two hours before we finished at the scene and returned to 14 Division.

"What do you think?" I asked "Billy the Brat" as he was affectionately known by the squad. Bill Kerr was a detective's detective and got the nickname due to his one hundred and eighty pounds of untamed fury! I was nicknamed "The Silver Fox" on account of my complete head of white hair. Cops always have nicknames for each other, it's just something we all do.

"I think it's pretty cut and dried," he answered, nodding his head.

"Looks like it," I agreed. "But we still have to dot our i's and cross our t's."

Back at 14 Division, we had a pretty good idea of what had transpired. Bill and I went into the interview room and found Edward Tolan was seated in a chair with his back to the north wall. Police Constable Keith Cowling stood by the door. Scott was in a second room providing a statement to the 14 Division detectives.

"Thanks officer, you can leave now," I told the uniform waiting with Tolan.

With that, Officer Cowling left the room, closing the door behind him. Detective Kerr and I sat at the only desk in the room.

"My name is Detective Bill McCormack, this is my

partner Detective Bill Kerr. We are from the Homicide Squad and we are investigating the death of Ann Price."

Tolan looked directly at me.

"I didn't kill her. I picked her up and carried her into the bedroom. I thought she had a seizure. We had an argument Sunday night but that was it, screaming and hollering you know. There was blood coming out of her nose and mouth just boom, all of a sudden."

I stopped him right there and told him he was under arrest. I then read him his rights and read him the standard caution. He answered that he understood. I then retrieved a typewriter from the outer office and placed a statement form in it.

"Can you tell me what happened tonight?" I asked him and began typing rapidly.

"Sunday night, I slapped her on the couch. I don't know what happened to her. The only time that I grabbed Ann was on Sunday night and I admit that. I wanted to know if she was living with Scott. That's the only time we had an argument. Can I call my lawyer?"

"Sure," I answered, "What's his name?" He gave me the name of his lawyer and I made the call for him. Tolan spoke to his lawyer in private for a few moments then returned to the interview room.

Edward Tolan was a large man. He was wearing purple pants and no shirt. His hands were swollen and blood stained and I noticed immediately that he had two tattoos on his arms, one on the left shoulder that said, "Cry here honey."

Tolan gave a formal statement reiterating the fact that he had gone out to get some wine and when he came back, he found Ann in a fetal position. He further stated that he had pounded her on the chest and given her mouth-to-mouth resuscitation then called the ambulance himself. "He did not kill her." What he gave us was an "exculpatory statement" which simply means that he was attempting to exonerate himself. It was painfully apparent that it was well rehearsed, beneficial only to himself under the circumstances and literally unbelievable. As a consequence, the supporting evidence from the autopsy and the witness statement told us a very different story.

We then took Tolan to Old City Hall where he was held on a charge of Murder, then made our way to the old morgue located at 86 Lombard Street where we met with the pathologist, Doctor Frank MacDonald. The post-mortem examination took just over an hour. Cause of Death: "Severe trauma to the body, aspiration of stomach contents and trauma of the head, consistent with a severe beating." Doctor MacDonald further stated that her injuries were that severe that she could have been mistaken for suffering a death equivalent to that of a car accident.

There wasn't a square inch of Anne's body that wasn't marked or traumatized. Her clothing was covered in black shoe polish, indentations of the frontal part of a man's shoe were located on the crotch area of her pants, indicative of a severe beating. The information we gathered at the autopsy was consistent with what Scott's statement had provided.

I then took possession of the clothing that had been worn by the deceased and Bill and I returned to headquarters. The investigation into the death of Ann Price was not a complicated one but we knew we would have to build the case with every piece of evidence we could find. We would not convict Edward Tolan on his statement. We were off to a good start with the statement that Scott Anderson had provided but in order to get a conviction, we needed a set of facts and or circumstances. The facts started to mount. All in all, nineteen articles were seized from the apartment, from the accused and from the victim.

These articles were sent to the Centre of Forensic Sciences where they were carefully analyzed and returned to us in the weeks to follow.

Shoes, pants and a shirt seized from the accused proved to have numerous human blood stains on them, the same blood type as Ann Price's. Many of the other exhibits came back with inconclusive results. We charged Tolan with the offense of Murder. I wasn't buying his story one bit, neither was Bill Kerr.

The trial was scheduled for April 2, 1975. The Crown Attorney was Robert McGee. It was learned from the defense that Tolan would be adhering to the fact that he was drunk at the time of the offence and thereby not responsible for the intent required for a murder conviction. He pleaded guilty to Manslaughter and was sentenced to fifteen years imprisonment. In less than ten years, he had committed two killings, pleaded guilty to two Manslaughter charges and served less than fifteen years total, in jail for both. He was out of jail by 1983.

As a police officer in today's society, I see far too much tragedy, far too many women killed in their own homes by the person they once trusted. We all can attest to this when on a daily basis, there are countless stories of domestic violence that continue to plague our society. Since this case, there have been several inquests, jury recommendations and guidelines put into place for police officers, yet, abusers continue to escalate the cycle of violence to the point of murder.

Homicide

"A killing of one human
being by another."

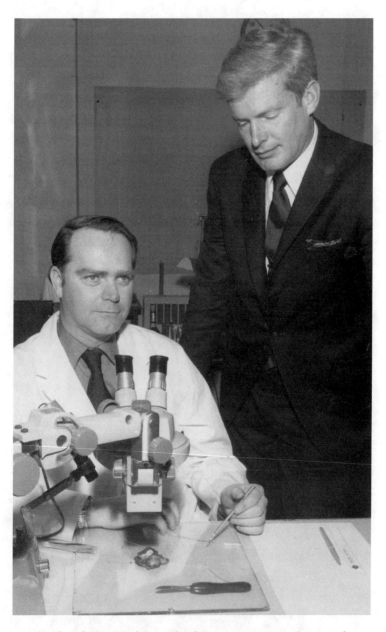

Dad with Fin Neilson, Chief Firearms expert, Centre of Forensic Science, examining a piece of evidence from a Homicide Scene.

CHAPTER THREE

LEONARD ROBERT GRAY

1975 WAS A DIFFICULT YEAR. I was fifteen and in my second year of high school. Mom was working full time as the Secretary at Bruce and Frankland Public Schools in Toronto.

This year brought both subtle and monumental changes to all our lives. It was the year my Grandfather died and the year my Grandmother came from Ireland to live with our mostly grown up family in an already overcrowded three bedroom, one-and-a-half bathroom home.

* * *

My father was born on the island of Mauritius in the Indian Ocean in 1933. He arrived into the world on the second floor of the only police station in the town that his family called home. His parents, William and Margaret were originally from Ireland but my grandfather, William Senior traveled to the island before World War Two to take over the position of First Class Sergeant Major in charge of Beau-Bassin Police Station. At the time, he held the lowest European rank of the British Colonial Police. During his tour in Mauritius, he was promoted to Inspector. My grandfather had signed a contract with the Colonial Police, which included a seven-month sabbatical in the United Kingdom every three years. In 1937, my grandparents took my father back home to Ireland for seven months.

Towards the end of 1937, the family returned to Mauritius. Grandfather was once again promoted, this time to the position of Chief Officer of Prisons, the equivalent rank to Chief Inspector in the Mauritius Police. In 1940, he took over the position of Commander of Field Forces that included the armed forces as well as the police. He was then promoted to Superintendent. When the war ended, my father's parents were ordered back to Britain so that my grandfather could take a course at Oxford University. The family moved to London, England for a short period until my grandfather could get himself established and then he moved my grand-mother and dad to Dublin where my dad attended school.

They returned to Mauritius a year later. My grandfather was awarded the MBE, (Member of the British Empire) for his work with Polio victims there. During his tenure with the Colonial Police, he had assisted with the invention of a leg brace for children struck down by Polio. He had also assisted with victims from two cyclones that had devastated the island during the war and was further rewarded for his contributions in assisting the British Empire.

The family lived in Mauritius until my grandfather retired in 1950, then were forced to leave the little island in the Indian Ocean that had become home and return to Ireland where my grandparents would remain until my grandfather's death. My grandparents bought land on the Liffey River near Dublin and my dad went back to school, graduated, and was appointed a sea-going radio officer by the Marcone International Communications Company Limited in the British Merchant Navy. He was immediately assigned as a radio officer on a troop ship and received a Korean Service Medal for his tour of duty.

After his tenure in the Navy, he joined the British Colonial Police in 1954, following closely in his father's footsteps. From there he went to Bermuda, another British colony and was a constable with the Bermuda Police for five years. This is where he met my mother, Jean. She was a Canadian who had traveled to Bermuda with her best friend, Bessie Bishop, to work for a few years. My parents met and were married in Bermuda. Quickly deciding that the island was too small to raise a family, they returned to Mom's hometown, Toronto. Dad resigned from his position and applied as a constable with the Metropolitan Toronto Police Force. He would feel at home in Canada, a former British colony, only this one had a lot less summer weather.

Before arriving in Toronto, they decided to take a short trip overseas to see my dad's parents. His folks hadn't met my mom. By then she was pregnant with their first grandchild. Bill junior was born in Ireland in June, 1959 and shortly after, Mom, Dad and baby were on their way to their new home. Toronto would be their last stop. My dad was hired by the Toronto Police and Mom remained pregnant for six years, t>6t>t>t>6

86 • KATHY CARTER

producing five offspring. During the sixties, my grandparents visited us in 1963. In 1968, Granddad came by himself for a three-week vacation that actually lasted six months. That was the one and only time in my life I got to meet him.

On October 9, 1975, my father got the fateful telephone call from overseas. His father had passed away in a hospital near Ballybrophy at the age of seventy-seven. It was a bad time. Dad and his cousin Pat flew home for the funeral. Pat had arrived in Toronto from Ireland in 1972 and after living with us for a couple of years, he also became a Toronto Police Officer. What we didn't know when Dad and Pat left, was that they'd be bringing back something. A gift more precious than any I'd experienced before. Dad brought home his mother, a woman I virtually never knew. My grandmother lived with us for a few years, before moving into her own apartment just up the street. She became more than a grandmother, she was a friend and confidant always there to help my father, especially when times got tough. I still miss her words of wisdom, her laughter, her candor and her charm.

1975 started off with a bang. My father was promoted to Staff Sergeant and was ending his partnership with fellow Staff Sergeant, Jack McBride. They had been partners in the Homicide Squad for the past few years but once promoted, it was the rule that two Staff Sergeants couldn't work together. Dad was assigned a junior Sergeant, new to the unit, Herman Lowe.

* * *

January was a busy month for the Homicide Squad in Toronto. By the end of the month, there had already been four murders. The death of Catherine Murphy on January 26th was Dad's second investigation that month.

Catherine Elizabeth Murphy was born in Scotland on August 28th, 1928. She came to Canada with her family and lived in several Canadian cities, finding trouble wherever she went. She was fifteen years old when she first came to the attention of the Police in Halifax, Nova Scotia and was sent to a reformatory where she escaped and roamed freely until she was caught and forced to return to finish her sentence. From Halifax, Catherine ended up in Ottawa, then Montreal and Kingston before finding herself in Toronto.

She was known to the police wherever she went, constantly finding herself with the wrong people on the wrong side of the law. All of her crimes revolved around money or drugs and she maintained a steady list of charges throughout her short life. She was out of prison on bail with Criminal Charges pending. Catherine married a few times, changing her last name after each union. Four children were born as a result of two of these marriages. She was forty-eight years old in 1975 at the time of her death.

Leonard Robert Gray was born in Toronto in December of 1929. He obtained a grade eight education and worked as a mechanic and also caught the odd job in a machine shop. He was married early in life, had two sons and later divorced. Leonard Gray first made his appearance in the criminal world in 1946 when he was seventeen years old. From that time, he too would be before the courts on a constant basis, spending the better part of his life in institutions and prisons. His record was a little more complex than Catherine's. Thefts, robberies, break-and-enters. Twice he was deported to Canada from the United States after finding himself in trouble there as well. In the early seventies, Leonard started upping the stakes, twice being charged with possessing firearms.

At the time of Catherine Murphy's death, Leonard Gray, "Bud" to his friends, was serving a three-year sentence in Joyceville Penitentiary, a high security correctional institution. He was transferred on October 21, 1974 after serving one third of his time to the Montgomery Centre in Toronto. The Montgomery Centre was a halfway house located on the southwest corner of Yonge and Montgomery Street, directly across from 53 Division. Leonard was granted day parole with the condition that he had to be back at the centre at night to report in.

It wasn't long before Catherine Murphy met up with Leonard Gray. Catherine often found herself in the company of criminals. On December 26, 1974, the day after Christmas, one of her friends, Henri Leschance was released from prison. He and Catherine had been friends for the last five years and were in the habit of shopping together, with stolen credit cards. Out of jail and nowhere to go, Henri found himself at Catherine's apartment. Together they decided that they should rent a second apartment, one to live in, one to stash stolen items. Henri introduced Catherine to another friend of his, Leonard Gray. They connected instantly.

On January 13, 1975, Catherine and Henri found a second apartment located at 2170 Gerrard Street East in the city's east end. The apartment Catherine rented was located in a three-story century-type home that still stands on the northwest corner of Gerrard Street and Enderby Road, two blocks west of Main Street, an area that hasn't changed much in the past twenty-five years. A quiet residential area, lined with shops of various types. One block north was Danforth Avenue and a shopping mall called "Shopper's World," that was within walking distance from the apartment. Streetcars still make their track both ways on Gerrard Street past the unassuming apartment complex.

They rented the apartment immediately and Catherine moved in the same day, using the name of M. Leschance. Satisfied that Catherine was comfortable in the new pad, Henri left, not wanting to interfere with the new relationship she had developed with his friend Leonard. Leonard began spending much of his "free" time with Catherine at the apartment. He brought the few possessions he owned, one being a handgun that he carried at all times. Leonard enjoyed playing with it and would often leave it out so that any visitors to the apartment would see it there. He was there to stay, even going as far as to rent a garage space for his car. A stolen car at that.

Within weeks, Catherine Murphy was back in business. Stolen credit cards. She and Leonard made their plans and were ready to put them into action. She had the two apartments, the one she had rented on Gerrard Street to live in and a second "safe house" where she would take the police if she ever got caught. The apartment she occupied on Gerrard Street would serve as the stash joint for the stolen property. On Saturday, January 25, 1975, Catherine and Leonard put their plan in motion. Two of Catherine's friends, Joan and Lisa met them around 3:00 p.m. at the Gerrard Street apartment. Catherine and Leonard were sorting the various credit cards, waiting for a telephone call to advise them the cards were working and could be used. At 3:10 p.m., the telephone rang. Catherine picked it up.

"Cards are good. Work fast." The caller hung up. The game was on.

"Okay, here's the plan," Leonard told the two girls. "You stay here and watch the place. I'll drop Cathy off and wait for her to get the goods and we'll all meet back here in a few hours."

"Sounds good," Catherine agreed. The other women nodded their heads.

Shortly after the couple left, the phone rang again. Lisa answered it. It was Leonard.

"Something's wrong," Leonard said.

"What's wrong?" Lisa asked him.

"Have you heard from Cathy?"

"No, why?" Lisa asked.

"I don't know, I lost her while we were working the cards and I went to a bar so I could use the phone. I think the cops must have got her."

Lisa was worried. Catherine was a good friend. "Oh no Leonard, what should we do?"

"I don't know. Maybe she'll show up. I'll call you back."

Leonard called back a few more times but there had been no calls, no sign of Catherine. At 6:45 p.m., Leonard arrived back at the apartment where Joan and Lisa were anxiously waiting.

"Did she come back?" He asked nervously, pacing up and down.

"No, not yet, no phone call either," Lisa answered.

"I'm telling you she got busted for the cards. I parked the car a few blocks away from here and walked back." Leonard crossed the floor to the window. Peeling back the drapes, he checked the street below. It was already dark, the street below deserted.

"She's going to bring the cops here, I just know it," Leonard stated, still nervous.

"I think if she got caught, she'd bring them to the other place." Lisa replied, confident of the original plan. "Why are you so worried?"

Leonard ignored her. "We've got to get some of this stuff out of here, clothes, jewelry. I don't want the cops finding it." Leonard started towards the bedroom.

Lisa crossed the room, opening the top drawer to a wooden chest. She held out her hand. "If there's anything we should get out of here it's these," six small bullets lay within her palm. "These are what you should be worried about."

Leonard took the bullets from her and threw them on the table. "Let me worry about them."

Lisa and Joan exchanged a silent expression of concern. "We're going to go now," Joan told Leonard. "Lisa and I haven't eaten and we're going to grab a quick bite. Tell Cathy to call us when she gets in." Both women headed for the door. Leonard watched as they disappeared behind it.

A few hours later, Joan and Lisa were in Lisa's apartment when the phone rang. It was Leonard. "Have you heard from her?"

"No, neither one of us has heard anything."

"Okay, thanks." Leonard Gray hung up the phone.

The two women were worried. "Something's wrong." Lisa said. "I can feel it." Joan told her not to worry.

* * *

The next day, Sunday, January 26, the landlord of the Gerrard Street building, Mrs. Foulds, decided to go to the apartment complex from her own home next door and check out apartment 3C as the tenants had moved out and she wanted to be sure the place was left clean. When she went into the washroom of 3C she observed what she thought was urine all over the walls, floor, toilet, sink and bathtub and heard the steady sound of something dripping. She looked up at the ceiling. The urine like substance was coming from the apartment directly above, 4B.

Mrs. Foulds ran up a flight of stairs to 4B and using her master key, she opened the door. She was immediately frozen by the sight of a female body lying right inside the door on the floor. Her eyes were open, a small black hole encrusted with dry blood was prominent over her left eye. Mrs. Foulds was dumbfounded. She didn't know what to do. It was the same woman who had rented the apartment some weeks before, that much she was sure of. She slowly lowered herself to her knees and touched the dead woman's wrist for a pulse. There was none. Without delay, she retreated from the scene, closing the door firmly behind her and ran to her apartment to call the police.

Constable George Smith was working the day shift at 55 Division, a fairly quiet division located at Coxwell and Dundas Streets. It had started out to be a routine Sunday but at 1:05 p.m. that changed. Constable Smith responded to a radio call to attend at 2170 Gerrard Street East. Arriving on the scene, he was met by Mrs. Foulds, the landlady, who took him immediately upstairs to apartment 4B. Constable Smith viewed the dead woman. "I'm going to need a few more officers here," he advised Mrs. Foulds.

Constable Roy Bradbury and Sergeant John Fitzgerald of 55 Division arrived on the scene within a couple of minutes. "I'll call the detectives," Fitzgerald stated. "You guys stay here, one with the body, the other at the front door."

"Got it," Bradbury responded.

Constable Ken Cenzura and Sergeant Dale Warriner were working in the Criminal Investigative Bureau of 55 Division. Ken Cenzura was an up and coming detective with ten years on the job. His regular partner, George McGivern was off on holidays so Ken paired up with Dale Warriner. This was to be

Ken Cenzura's first homicide investigation. He would, later in his career, go on to work in the Homicide Squad for nine years. A move that modeled two of his mentors, Bill McCormack and Jack McBride.

Cenzura and Warriner got the call at around 1:10 p.m. and rushed to the scene. Constable Bradbury was situated at the front door of the building when the two detectives arrived. He immediately wrote down both officers' names and recorded the time of their arrival in his memo book.

"It's up on the third floor. Apartment 4B," Bradbury told the detectives.

"Thanks." They all looked at their watches, synchronizing the time – 1:35 p.m. They were within a minute of each other which would be noted so their evidence would be consistent in court.

Cenzura and Warriner took the rear stairs to the third floor. From the hallway, Cenzura could clearly see an open door with the letters 4B on it and on the floor, just inside the door, he saw the outline of a woman's body. She was lying on her back, dressed in a blue checked pantsuit. It appeared that she had been dead for some time due to the absence of color from her skin and the odor that was beginning to foul the air.

"Who found her?" Cenzura asked Constable Smith. Constable Smith and the ambulance attendants had remained in the apartment.

"Landlady. Mrs. R. Foulds. She lives across the way." Smith said.

Cenzura knelt down to examine the body further. Her left eye was closed, a streak of blood ran down her face from a tiny hole just above her eyebrow. It was a clean wound. He noted everything about her and her positioning in his book. Standing, he took in the contents of the apartment. It appeared clean, a single vase was knocked over in the corner, other than that, the place was relatively orderly.

"What do you think?" Cenzura turned to his partner. Warriner was also writing.

"What do I think? I think I should call homicide and let them know what we've got."

"Good idea. Where's the closest phone?" Cenzura asked.

"Right across the hallway." Constable Smith pointed to the closed door that faced 4B.

"Okay, I'll go call," Warriner stated, "Smith, you stay here with the body, Ken, see what you can get from the landlady, I'll be over in a minute."

With that, Dale Warriner knocked loudly on the doorway of Apartment 4C. It was answered by an elderly woman who allowed him to use the phone. Cenzura headed for the stairway, leaving the uniformed officer with the deceased.

The information Constable Cenzura and Sergeant Warriner obtained from the landlady would be of great assistance to the investigation. So far, they had no identification on the girl and nothing at all on a possible suspect. Mrs. Foulds told the officers that the apartment had been rented to a married couple, Henri and Marie Leschance. However, a few weeks after they moved in, Mrs. Foulds was awakened at 4:00 a.m. one morning by the sound of loud knocking on her door. When she answered the door, it was not Mr. Leschance standing there but another man who claimed to be Marie's husband. He identified himself as Mr. Gray and said he had locked himself out of the apartment. Mrs. Foulds was immediately suspicious and asked who Leschance was. Gray responded that that was the name his wife used but he was in fact her husband.

Mrs. Foulds let him into the apartment. On her way back to her own complex, she saw a strange car parked at the rear of the building. It was a Ford Limited. She had seen the car there on numerous occasions and had once seen Mr. Gray park it and enter the building next door, the building that Catherine Murphy lived in. She wrote down the plate number and kept it on a piece of paper. A piece of paper she now handed to Constable Cenzura.

* * *

Sunday January 26, 1975 was a regular working day for Staff Sergeant Jack McBride and Staff Sergeant Bill McCormack. My father had been promoted to Staff Sergeant and would soon be assigned to a new partner. Dad and Jack McBride had worked together for three years. When the call came in from Sergeant Warriner at 1:40 p.m., Jack looked straight at his partner.

"Looks like we've got one more, Bill." He hung up the phone. Both men exchanged a reluctant, knowing glance. It was to be their last murder investigation together. A case that particularly sticks out in Dad's memory and this is how he relates it.

* * *

"Where are we going Jack?" I asked my partner, glancing at my watch to have the exact time of departure from Police Headquarters.

"2170 Gerrard Street East. It's not too far. We can probably get there in fifteen to twenty minutes."

"Okay, what's up?" I pulled out a pad of foolscap from the top drawer of my desk, ready to take down times, dates and addresses.

"Female found lying just inside apartment 4B. Looks like

a gunshot. Single shot to the head," McBride answered, reaching for his coat, as he relayed the rest of the information.

"Let's go."

Gulping down the last of my cold coffee, I grabbed the set of car keys from the hook above the desk and Jack and I were on our way. We arrived on the scene at 1:59 p.m. Sergeant Fitzgerald and Constable Bradbury directed us to where Constable Smith was waiting in apartment 4B.

The hallway was deserted, the door to apartment 4B slightly ajar as we entered. Taking detailed notes is one of the most essential parts of any investigation. I immediately began writing down everything I saw, position of the furniture, positioning of the body, contents of a spilled purse, etc. When it was time to examine the body, I snapped on a pair of surgical gloves that I kept in my back pocket.

By this time, Sergeant Roy Gosby of the Identification Bureau had arrived and began photographing the scene. The Coroner, Doctor Robson arrived shortly after and examined the body. He pronounced her dead and ordered a post-mortem examination that would occur immediately after her removal to the morgue at East General Hospital.

"Let's get to work Jack," I said. By this time, Jack McBride had also pulled on a pair of latex gloves. Meticulously, we went through every bit of evidence, bagging, numbering and labeling each item we recovered, lamps, a worn out woman's wallet, swabs of blood and other body fluids. After an hour had passed, the pathologist, Doctor Hutson arrived. He also took notes of the body and the wound.

Cenzura and Warriner were back within the hour and the four of us shook hands. It was Ken Cenzura's first encounter with the legendary McCormack and McBride and later said it was one that immediately impressed him.

"Got some information from the landlady," Cenzura informed.

"Okay, what do you have so far?" McBride took out his blue memo book and turned to the first blank page.

"She wrote down the plate number of a car that's been parked here a few times in the last couple of weeks. I ran it, comes back stolen. She gave us a pretty good description of the man driving it. Says he's the husband of the deceased, at least that's what he told her. Different name than hers though. This guy goes by the name of 'Gray'. Dale and I are going to go back to the office, see what we can dig up."

"Sounds good," McBride nodded, scribbling the information quickly into his book. The apartment was now swarming with detectives, doctors and uniformed officers. All going about their business, the business of collecting and cataloguing evidence, putting together the pieces of a broken puzzle.

At approximately 4:50 p.m., the telephone in the apartment started to ring.

"Has the phone been printed?" I asked Gosby.

"Yup, it's safe now," he replied. The prints had been lifted by the technicians so there was no worry about mine contaminating the evidence.

"Can you pick that up?" I nodded at the telephone to Sergeant King who had just come up from the front entrance.

"Sure." He picked it up on the fourth ring.

"Hello."

"Who's this?" It was a female voice.

"This is Sergeant King from Toronto Police. Who may I ask is this?"

"Sergeant King?" The caller was confused. "What are you doing in Cathy's apartment?"

"I can answer you that when you tell me who you are and what your relationship is to Cathy." King stated.

"My name is Lisa." The caller identified herself. "Cathy Murphy is a friend of mine. She lives there. Is everything okay?"

"When is the last time you saw her?" King asked.

"Saturday. I was worried, I haven't seen her since then."

"Is there anyway you could come to 55 Division to speak to us today?" King asked, not wanting to deliver bad news over the phone.

"I don't know, possibly. What's it concerning." Lisa was worried. She didn't want to get involved with the police, not with what she knew about her friend Cathy and Leonard.

King had a feeling that the caller might not comply with his request so he delivered the news. "I'm sorry to have to tell you this, your friend Cathy is dead."

Silence.

"What time do you want me at the station?" Lisa finally asked. Cathy was dead. She was sure Leonard had something to do with it.

"Whatever time is convenient for you," King replied.

"I'll be there by five," she said and hung up.

"Potential witness, named Lisa." King told us.

"That's great. Ken, you and Dale see what you can get from her. Jack and I will go to the hospital for the autopsy, we'll meet you back at 55 Division as soon as we can," I told them.

"Don't think we'll be home in time for dinner tonight." Jack remarked as he occupied the passenger seat.

"We'll be lucky if we're home for breakfast!"

The autopsy was performed by Doctor Hutson, the same pathologist who attended the scene. We arrived at the morgue for the procedure at 5:10 p.m. and it was completed by 7:30 p.m. Cause of death: Gunshot wound to the head.

Ken Cenzura and Dale Warriner were waiting for us. They had been busy, rounding up and interviewing witnesses, checking names, license plates and occurrences on the computer system. The deceased woman was Catherine Murphy. Officers were on their way to notify her family. Slowly, we began to put the pieces of the story together and through it all, the suspect, Leonard Gray began to emerge. We learned that he had stolen a vehicle earlier that week.

We also learned that Gray had been incarcerated and only through further investigation, discovered that he was presently out on parole and had been staying at the Montgomery Centre, a halfway house on Yonge Street for paroled criminals.

It would be a long night of interviewing witnesses, writing reports, examining physical evidence and putting together all the information required to obtain a warrant of arrest for Leonard Gray. Trays of coffee and half packages of cigarettes littered the tops of the desks throughout the office. By 10:30 a.m. on Monday, January 27, we went before a Justice of the Peace at the courts in Old City Hall to swear out a warrant that charged Leonard Gray with the murder of Catherine Murphy.

That done, Jack and I went home, but not for long.

At about 4:00 p.m. on Sunday, January 26, 1975, Leonard "Bud" Gray had arrived at a friend's apartment in Hamilton, Ontario, about an hour and a half drive west from Toronto. Ditching the stolen Ford in a vacant lot outside the complex, he walked quickly from the car through the unlocked door to his friend's apartment. Leonard was in luck, he found his friend Peter at home. Gray needed a place to stay and Peter offered the companionship of a female acquaintance. Leonard took him up on it immediately.

It was after 11:00 p.m. before he found himself in a small one-bedroom apartment atop an Italian Restaurant in downtown Hamilton. His new companion, Laura was very accommodating. She gave Leonard a pillow and blanket and showed him to the couch where he spent the night. It was late Monday afternoon before he woke up and Laura had already been down to the restaurant to pick up food for dinner. The two ate in silence in front of her television in the living room.

Biting down on her last piece of pasta, Laura noted a shiny object lying on the couch beside Leonard.

"What is that?" she asked, pointing to it.

"Oh that, that's a gun." Leonard answered. "I don't go anywhere without it."

"Could you please put it away?" Laura asked. She was nervous, had never seen a real gun before.

"Sure. No problem." Leonard answered, picking up the gun and slipping it into his belt.

The sound of the phone startled Laura. She picked it up after a few rings. The man on the other end identified himself as a police officer. Alarmed, Laura hung up. Trouble was on the way, she could feel it.

Sergeant Jack Sutton and Sergeant Jim Garchinski of the Hamilton Wentworth Police Force were working the afternoon shift on Monday January 27, 1975. The Detectives in the Toronto Homicide Squad had been busy and had traced Gray to an address in Hamilton. Sutton took the call from Staff Sergeant McBride. The information was legit, Cenzura and Warriner had located Gray's friend Peter in Hamilton. Peter wanted no trouble with the law and told the detectives where they could find Gray. Hamilton Police were to attend at an apartment on Barton Street to locate him.

"Tell your guys to be careful, he's armed. We haven't recovered the gun," McBride told Detective Sutton.

"Is there a warrant?" Sutton asked, writing down every bit of information, descriptions of the accused, the vehicle, the gun.

"Yup. Swore to it this morning. Canada wide for murder. Let us know what you come up with," McBride finished, leaving his number with Sutton.

"Will do." Sutton hung up the phone and turned to his partner.

"We're on. Let's get some back-up."

The detectives were well aware of the location they had to visit. It was an Italian restaurant on Barton Street across the road from an elementary school. Barton Street is located on the northeastern side of Hamilton, close to the industrial area of town. The area hasn't changed much since 1975, mostly single dwelling homes and shops, a few small strip malls line the street front.

Within minutes, Sutton and Garchinski had assembled a team. They would have to call on detectives from across the city, Hamilton Mountain, Central Division and the East End. In 1975 there were no Emergency Task Forces to call on, the detectives were it. They would arrange themselves to do takedowns with the officers who had the youngest families at home forming up at the rear of the line. The thinking was that the first in had the greatest chance of being shot or killed. Four of the officers assembled, Detectives Ryan, Sutton, Garchinski and Wallace had recently taken a Hostage Negotiator Course. The Hamilton Wentworth Police Force were attempting to bring their officers up to date after the 1972 hostage taking at the Munich Olympics. This was the first time they might have to use it.

The team included Sergeant Ronald Bond, Staff Sergeant Worth and Sergeant Duffy. Sure of their information, they had to move fast. They knew that Gray was not alone and they were unsure of his status with the female who rented the premises. Together with a contingent of uniformed officers, they arrived at the apartment. Surrounding the entrance as best they could, the officers took up tactical positions in the hallway.

"COME OUT OF THERE GRAY, WE KNOW YOU'RE IN THERE, IT'S THE POLICE!"

Laura came to the door. Opening it a crack, she observed the officers in the hallway, guns out, pointed directly at her. "He's not here," she said timidly.

"Where is he?" Sergeant Bond demanded.

"In the bathroom." As she was answering, Leonard Gray appeared at the doorway, his hands extended.

"Don't shoot!" Gray pushed the door open and walked toward the officers, hands up.

"Get down on the floor!" Garchinski ordered, his gun pointed directly at Gray's chest.

Gray lay face down on the floor and Sergeant Duffy went forward quickly, pinning Gray to the ground with his knee while he snapped the handcuffs on him. Gray was mumbling, mostly to himself but loud enough for the officer's to hear what he was saying.

"Why don't you do it to me, man?" he asked.

Sutton ignored his statement. "Where's the gun?" Detective Bond asked.

"I threw it away." Gray answered. Detective Bond reached into Gray's pocket. He turned it inside out and the contents spilled onto the floor. A pocketknife, small change and fourteen .22 caliber live shells. "I'm going to ask you again. Where's the gun?" Bond continued searching.

"I told you, I threw it away. Why don't you guys just give it to me? Shoot me now."

"We don't operate that way." Bond replied. "Get him out of here."

Gray was led away in cuffs. Sutton phoned Toronto Police. After an intensive search of the apartment, the gun was found by Sergeant Dave Wallace under the vanity in the bathroom. It was a .22 caliber revolver with a cut off barrel. The barrel had been cut short so that it could be easily concealed in a pocket. In the kitchen, Sergeant Barby located a man's jacket thrown over a trunk. Eighty-five shells were found in the front pocket. The evidence was seized, mission accomplished.

After a quick dinner and visit with my family, Jack McBride and I were on our way again. I got called at home by the Hamilton Police around 9:30 p.m. on the 27 of January. They had our man. I met Jack at headquarters at 10:00 p.m. and we were off to Hamilton. We arrived at the Central Police Station around 11:30 p.m. where we met with Sergeant Jack Sutton and Sergeant Jim Garchinski. Gray was seated in a small interview room. He was disheveled, shaking his head from side to side.

Jack and I went in and slid two chairs across the desk from Gray. I pulled out my pad of foolscap as well as a blank statement sheet.

"I'm Staff Sergeant McCormack, this is my partner Staff Sergeant McBride. We're from the Metropolitan Toronto Police Homicide Squad." I then read Gray his rights.

Gray looked up at us and nodded that he understood. "What is your name?" I asked.

"Leonard Robert Gray."

"Do you go by any other name?"

"Yeah," he answered, "I go by Bud."

"You are arrested on a charge of murder. On Sunday, January 26, 1975 at about 12:45 p.m. the dead body of Mrs.

Catherine Murphy was found at her apartment at 2170 Gerrard Street East in Toronto. What, if anything, do you wish to tell me about this matter?"

Leonard Gray started crying. "I didn't mean to kill her. I wish there was some way I could make you kill me. I'm going to jail for the rest of my life. I loved the chick, I loved her." Gray was sobbing uncontrollably.

"Is there anything else you wish to say?"

He shook his head. The interview was over.

The trial for Leonard Robert "Bud" Gray started on November 17, 1975. The Crown Attorney assigned to the case was Clair Lewis, an up and coming attorney and well versed in the law.

Leonard Gray on the other hand opted to go with Legal Aid as he couldn't afford a lawyer. His case was given to the firm of Pomerant/Pomerant and Greenspan. A young Edward Greenspan was assigned to take it on. Greenspan looked over the facts. It was an open and shut case, a no win. He decided to hand it over to the junior man of the firm, Michael Moldaver and an articling student, Casey Hill. It was to be Mike Moldaver's first murder case.

There wasn't a lot to go with from the start. After meeting with his client several times, Moldaver got the story from him that he would later relate in court. Gray came home that night after going back to search for Cathy at the mall. She was waiting in the apartment for him. She thought the police were coming for them and when Leonard opened the door, Cathy was standing there with the gun in her hand. Relieved to see him, she flung her arms around him and the gun went off, instantly killing her. Leonard decided to run. What else could he do? The cops would never believe him, not with his record, that it had been an accidental shooting.

Mike Moldaver had his work cut out for him. He would

have to get a jury to believe this story. It wouldn't be easy. The first course of business was to make his client's appearance acceptable to the court. Leonard Gray had never owned a suit in his life. Moldaver took his client from his office on Bay Street over to the Simpson's store that was then located at the corner of Yonge and Queen Streets in downtown Toronto.

"We have to make you look presentable," Moldaver told Gray, walking him into the men's section of the store.

"Mr. Moldaver, I don't have the money for a suit," Gray stated, looking down at his shoes. Pretty much everything he owned he had stolen from somewhere or obtained with stolen credit cards.

"Don't worry about it. This one's on me," Mike told him.

Picking out a plain blue suit, tie and shirt for his client, the last step was to get him to try it on.

"I'll wear the suit Mr. Moldaver, but I won't wear a tie. I can't stand to have anything around my neck."

"Okay. That's fine," Moldaver agreed. He paid for the clothing.

I was told by my father that the trial for Leonard Gray was not unusually long. The cards were stacked in the Crown's favor and Mike Moldaver knew it. It was common knowledge in the law community that it was near suicide to go after Bill McCormack on the stand. He was a defense lawyer's nightmare. He had the good looks and charm of a Hollywood movie star and was extremely apt at winning over most juries. He was confidant, and methodical and could not be swayed with innuendos and supposition. Moldaver cross-examined his evidence, but made it short and sweet. Trying to attack Dad's creditability or testimony was not the way to win the case.

As it turned out, the way to win it came through the pathologist and the accused himself. At the preliminary hearing some months earlier, the pathologist testified that he had wiped the wound on Catherine Murphy's face with a wet cloth. At the trial, he testified that he had wiped the wound with a dry cloth. The significance of this statement was that the pathologist contradicted himself and cast doubt on the fact that there could have been gunpowder residue around the wound. A dry cloth may have picked up evidence of gunpowder residue, which would be consistent with the accused version of events.

If in fact a wet cloth had been used, it would have verified the Crown's account, that it was Leonard Gray in the apartment with the gun and when Cathy came through the door, it was he who thought it was the police. He then shot at her from a distance, one round striking her above the left eye, killing her instantly. A wet cloth would have been used by the pathologist only if he did not suspect or observe any evidence of gunpowder.

* * *

When Gray took the stand, he broke down several times, repeating over and over again that it was an accident and he loved Cathy. He had nothing left to live for.

The jury retired with all the facts on the 24th of November. Mike Moldaver went home. After the jury was out for six hours Mike got a call from Eddie Greenspan.

"Looks good Mike. The longer they're out the better. Want to give me the case back?" He joked.

"Not likely. This one is all mine," he hung up the phone.

During their deliberations, the jury once again asked for the ballistic report. After giving them this information, the judge in the case, re-charged the jury on the issue of reasonable doubt. Reasonable doubt being a set of facts or circumstances that would lead a normally prudent or cautious

person to have a strong belief that goes beyond mere sus-
picion. This infuriated the Crown Attorney, Clair Lewis and
he strongly objected to the judge's words but to no avail. The
jury came back with their verdict. "Not Guilty."

Leonard Gray did his best to try to keep a low profile after
the trial but it wasn't long before he was in trouble again. Two
years later, in the early hours of May 3, 1977 he was arrested
and charged by officers at 13 Division for theft of a cheque
and credit card. The officers checked his record and decided
that they would keep him in the cells until he could attend a
bail hearing before a Justice of the Peace that morning.

He was placed in a monitored cell. The holding cells at 13
Division were state of the art. The new station had opened up
in 1974 and was outfitted with the most modern cell moni-
toring equipment available at the time. These cameras had
been installed so that officer's could watch the prisoners in the
cell area on a closed circuit television from the front desk.
However, within ten minutes of being lodged, Gray was dead.
Taking the shirt he was wearing, he lay down on the floor of
the cell, just under where the camera focused and tied the shirt
to the cell bars. He then wrapped it around his neck and
leaned into it until he strangled to death. The man who
refused to wear a tie was dead by his own hand.

Malice

"Desire to see another suffer that may be fixed and unreasonable or no more than a passing mischievous impulse; intent to commit an unlawful act or cause harm without legal justification or excuse."

Dad and pathologist assistant, Chris Heck - Coroner's Office.

CHAPTER FOUR

WILLIAM MARVIN ROBERT WILLSIE

APRIL 1977, I was nearing the end of Grade eleven, comfortable in my life at Notre Dame High School with my friends, Maire, Teresa and Donna, co-conspirators in every venture. Looking back now, it's easy to see just how great life was. One more year of high school then we'd be going our separate ways, one to college, one to work, one remaining for grade thirteen, then off to university. It would be a new beginning for each of us, but also an end to four years of bonding, building trust, friendships. It was like that for my dad too. He was coming to the end of his run in the Homicide Squad, a place where he also bonded with his fellow investigators, building trusts, respect and friendships that are still valuable today.

* * *

had watched my father and his close police friends since I had been a child and I knew that being a cop was what I really wanted. I had no idea how my dad felt about this. After graduating from high school, I spent that summer working part time, and traveling with my family to Florida for our annual vacation.

One particularly hot July afternoon, my dad and I went out into the Gulf of Mexico on a four man yellow rubber dingy, fishing for sharks. I loved spending this time with him, just the two of us, away from my siblings. I dropped my line under the waves and let my feet dangle in the turquoise water.

"I was thinking about putting my application in when we get back," I ventured.

Dad cut a piece of bait, expertly fastening it to the end of his hook. He cast it overboard.

"You're only seventeen," he answered without looking up.

"I could apply for cadet." I'd already thought it through.

"I guess you could," he agreed, "but I'm not sure that this would be the right thing for you."

"Why not?" I asked.

"It's not a great job for a woman you know, you'll get sent to the youth bureau or parking."

"That's okay with me," I told him. "I'll work wherever they want me to."

He reeled in his untouched bait. "I don't know," he sighed, "why do you want to do this?"

I thought for a second before I answered. "Dad, I've always wanted to do this. I know it's more a man's world than a woman's but it's in me. I can't think about spending my life behind a desk somewhere. I see what you do, I want to be out there, solving crimes, putting together the pieces. I've known it since I was a kid."

He smiled, pulling his hat over his brow to block the sun. "You don't know how much I'll worry."

"Probably not, but you know I'll do it anyway."

"That much I do know," he relented.

Before going to college that September, I applied to the Metropolitan Toronto Police for the position of cadet. It would be almost two years before I heard back from them, a hiring freeze had delayed my application, but once the ball was rolling, it never stopped.

Leaving the Homicide Squad in 1977 was the furthest thing from my father's mind, but move from there he would. One naturally assumes when you get good at something and enjoy it, you'll be there forever, but there is one sure thing that you can always rely on and that is that things change. Constantly. I was hired as a Cadet and my dad moved out of Homicide forever.

* * *

Friday, April 1, 1977 would bring about a fatal change for a young woman named Linda Peagram or as she was known to her friends, Amanda (Mandy) Leigh St. John. At about 10:25 p.m. that night, she was stabbed to death at "Larry's Hideaway Hotel" in downtown Toronto.

Amanda Leigh St. John was born in St. Catherine's, Ontario. In her short life of twenty-seven years, she had gone by several other names, one from a failed marriage and several others because they suited her. She had five children, four living, the youngest dead from leukemia.

She was the daughter of a police officer and an only child. In 1974, she moved to Toronto and was often seen in the downtown area of the city where she frequented various hotels on a nightly basis.

Amanda met different men at these hotels. Once the connection was made, they would make arrangements for a room at another hotel, and then meet at this destination. She made sure she left each hotel alone and met the "flavor of the night" at another location, allowing her the opportunity to "bow out" if she didn't feel right about the trick. She rarely brought a man home.

Amanda was a good-looking girl, tall and slim. She had long brown hair and striking blue eyes. Amanda never appeared in the short skirts or tight clothing usually associated with girls of her trade, but made a point of wearing the latest styles. Outside her profession she kept a good lifestyle and home for her four children, one of which attended a private school in downtown Toronto. What she did at work was kept separate, but the income was keeping Amanda in the lifestyle she desired.

Mandy kept mostly to herself when plying her trade but still got along well with the other prostitutes that frequented the downtown area.

On the night of April 1, 1977, at about 6:30 p.m., she went to the Warwick Hotel. In those days, the Warwick was located on the northwest corner of Dundas and Jarvis Streets in the heart of downtown Toronto at the border of 52 and 51 Divisions. The hotel has long since been torn down, a parking lot and the Sears building are all that remain close to the site. At that time, the Warwick was a beehive of activity. A hotel complete with a coffee shop and a noisy red-lit basement lounge where one could have a drink, watch a girl strip or simply listen to nightly entertainment.

The Warwick Hotel housed twenty-five to thirty prostitutes on a good day. Girls ranged in age from eighteen to fifty, some were high school dropouts, runaways and some university students. The girls would come to the hotel, sit alone nursing a drink at a table and wait for the connection, the trick. Once the connection was made, they would usually take their business to another establishment away from the Warwick, but would be back within a couple of hours for another.

This was how it was on the night of April Fool's Day, 1977 for Mandy St. John. She had already been in and out of the Warwick twice that night. She was last seen there before 9:00 p.m., making further arrangements for the evening and was seen leaving the hotel at 9:30 p.m.

At 10:00 p.m. the same night, Amanda entered the lobby of Larry's Hideaway, a short distance away. This was her third time in the place that evening. Larry's Hideaway was located on the south side of Carlton Street, a few blocks east of Jarvis Street. It was a small hotel, with a bar that sometimes hosted singers and bands.

Mandy approached the clerk on duty, Gerry Bannon and asked if there was a "Bob" in room 225. Gerry knew Amanda, she was quiet, pretty, never gave him any trouble. He called the room but there was no answer. Amanda waited by the desk for a few minutes. Gerry noticed that she was well dressed and appreciated her good looks.

"Nice coat," he remarked, breaking the silence, scanning the silver jacket she wore. The jacket came mid thigh and actually glistened like asbestos.

"Thanks," Amanda shot back, impatiently eyeing her watch.

Just then, the telephone at the desk rang and Bannon was momentarily distracted with another customer. When he completed his call, he looked up to the place he had last seen the girl in the nice coat but she was gone. He didn't know at the time but he would be one of the last people to see her alive.

William Marvin Robert Willsie was forty-seven years old.

Originally from Windsor, he had no permanent address in
Toronto. William Willsie was an average looking man, slightly
overweight and balding. He wore thick-framed black horned
rimmed glasses that had been in style during the Buddy Holly
years.

William Willsie had been in and out of trouble his entire
life. Nothing major, small petty crimes like theft and forgery.
Having had enough of Canada at the age of twenty-two, he
decided to head for the United States for a while, got into
trouble, and was deported from Mobile, Alabama after
authorities arrested him. Over the next fifteen-year period, he
would continue his cycle of petty thefts and forgeries and
spend time in and out of Kingston Penitentiary. On April 1,
1977, William Willsie was living at the Salvation Army Hostel
on Sherbourne Street, unemployed and on welfare.

He arrived at Larry's Hideaway at approximately 8:45 p.m.
that night. He asked for a room and was handed the key to
room number 225. He paid for the room in cash, eleven
dollars and seventy-five cents plus a one-dollar deposit for the
key. He placed the key in his pocket and made his way down
the hallway.

At 9:15 p.m. that night, clerk Gerry Bannon received a
phone call from a woman. She asked if a Bob Wilson had
checked in.

"As a matter of fact, he checked in less than an hour ago,"
Gerry informed her.

"Good, what room is he in?" she asked.

"225. Would you like me to connect you?" Gerry asked.

"No thanks."

The line went dead.

Gerry hung up. He didn't give the call much thought.
That sort of thing went on a lot at this place. He went about
his routine until about ten when he saw Amanda St. John enter

the lobby. The fact that he didn't see her leave didn't bother him either. That also went on here as well. He knew the game they all played and stayed out of it. He was hired to rent rooms, period.

Not even a half hour had passed when Gerry got a buzz at the front counter for two rooms calling at the same time. Rooms 223 and 225. He decided to answer 223 first. He picked up the phone and immediately recognized the voice. It was "Janine" a girl he had booked into that room several times.

"What's up?" he asked into the receiver.

"Gerry, there's something going on in the room next door. I can hear someone screaming!"

The buzzer continued for room 225. One thing Gerry knew for sure, if the buzzer was going, there was trouble. The girls that frequented this establishment had a code with the staff. If there was any trouble at all with any of the customers, they would knock the phone off the hook and it would immediately buzz the front desk. The clerk on duty would know something was up.

Gerry listened, still connected to room 223. He could hear the screaming too. It was a woman's voice. The shrill tone echoed through the receiver. "Please no! Oh, my God." Immediately, Gerry plugged into room 225, the second one that had buzzed him at the same time. He could hear the screams clearly. "Oh, my God! Oh, my God!"

Gerry pressed the button on his control panel that sent an alert to the bar area. As soon as the girl in the bar answered he told her he needed help right away, send the bouncers.

Mark Leone, John Stewart and Ted Stilson were working that night. They got to the main lobby as quickly as they could.

"We got trouble in room 225," he told them when they arrived.

"What kind of trouble?" Mark asked.

"I don't know, a girl's screaming. Room 225," Gerry answered, handing Mark the passkey to the door.

"We'll look after it," Mark re-assured him. Together, the three men ran down the hall, Gerry tagged along to see what was happening. Arriving at the door, they paused momentarily, listening for sounds from inside. Mark knocked heavily on the closed door. A man opened it immediately. He was dressed only in his pants but his arms were covered in blood. The man walked out of the room into the hallway, leaving the door slightly ajar.

"I did it, I'm guilty, take me in, arrest me," he shouted, placing his hands out in front of him, expecting the men to handcuff him. Instead, Mark Leone and John Stewart pushed the door of the room open further to get a better look inside, totally unprepared for the scene they were about to witness.

The girl inside the room was naked, covered in blood. There was blood on the walls, carpet, even on the door. The bed was disheveled, sheets and blankets lay in a heap on top of the mattress, heavily soaked with a red sticky substance. The girl had been lying on the bed on her front when they walked in. She stood up, making an attempt to get to the door where the men waited, unsure of what to do next. The knife was still protruding from the center of her back, it's brown handle covered with blood. She held her hands out to the men for help and tried to talk but stumbled and turned back to the bed where she collapsed, her right hand on the receiver of the phone.

"Quick, get an ambulance!" Mark ordered.

Bannon ran down the hall, and called the police and an ambulance. The man with the blood soaked hands waited quietly in the hall.

"Can I have a smoke?" he asked John, unwavering,

apparently unaffected by the activity going on around him. John Stewart pulled out a lighter and lit a cigarette for him. William Willsie inhaled deeply, letting the smoke fill his lungs. "Thanks," he said, leaning back on the wall. Mark came out of the room.

"Get back in there," he ordered Willsie. "I don't want you going anywhere. Watch him," Mark told John. Willsie did what he was told. Mark ran to the front, told Gerry to put a rush on the ambulance and secured the bar area. When he got back, he went back to the room. Willsie was by the window, picking up his clothes from the ledge.

"Put those down, you aren't going anywhere," Mark commanded. Willsie again did what he was told.

Police Constables Stephen Craig and Barbara Buchanan were working the afternoon shift in 52 Division. They got a radio call to help out at "Larry's Hideaway Hotel" for a possible stabbing. Constable Craig and Buchanan arrived at the hotel a few minutes later. It was 10:28 p.m.

As they entered the lobby, a man yelled out to them from down the hallway.

"Over here officers, it's a bad one, he's still in there with her, room 225." He pointed to the hallway on the west side of the building. When Constable Buchanan opened the door, she saw William Willsie. He was leaning against the north wall, just inside the doorway. On the bed, lying crossways, feet to the south, was a naked female, face up. She was covered in blood, her arms over her head and a telephone receiver was cradled in her right hand. Constable Buchanan rushed to her side. She detected eye movement but could not feel a pulse.

Constable Craig placed Willsie under arrest for attempted murder and advised him of his rights. Placing his hands to the rear, Constable Craig then put the suspect in handcuffs.

"Where's the weapon?" Constable Buchanan asked.

"It's in her back, the knife is still in her back," Willsie replied matter-of-factly.

Back-up arrived. Police Constable John Shulga and Randy Power were next on the scene. Their job would be to secure the room, making sure no one came in or out. Constable Craig took Willsie out of the room and secured him in room 222. It was time to call the Homicide Squad.

Ambulance crew arrived within minutes and took Amanda St. John with the knife still plunged deep into her back to Wellesley Hospital, a short trip away. Constables Larry McCoy and John Bills from 51 Division had also arrived on scene and volunteered to go to the hospital with the victim.

Back in room 222, Willsie was seated on a freshly made bed. Constable Craig read him the standard caution. Willsie stated that he understood and gave his full name. William Robert Marvin Willsie.

Constable Craig asked him for his date of birth and address. He provided his birth date, stating simply that he stayed at the "Sally Anne." Constable Buchanan entered the room after the victim was removed to hospital. Constable Craig looked up as she entered the room, lifting his eyebrows questioningly. She answered with a shrug of her shoulders, not knowing if Amanda St. John would survive or not. Constable Craig continued his questioning of the accused.

"Is there anything that you wish to tell me about what happened in room 225?" His notebook was in his hand, pen ready.

Willsie looked up at him from the bed. "All I know is that she tried to rob me. That's all I know. If she hadn't tried to steal my money, everything would have been all right. I only had about twenty dollars, what the hell would she want with eighteen or nineteen lousy bucks? You pay a woman fifty bucks and then she tries to steal your last few bucks. I warned her! I told her, 'Sweetheart, don't fucking do it!' I told her, 'Don't do it baby!' When she tried to steal my money, the funny thing is, she had the knife."

"Let's get him out of here," Craig told his partner.

William Willsie was loaded into the scout car and transported to 51 Division where they would wait for the Homicide Squad detectives to arrive. It was now after 11:00 p.m. The two officers brought the accused to the second floor of the old station, took off one handcuff and sat him in the chair, snapping the handcuffs in front.

"Thanks, that's better," he said smiling.

He then carried on with his story.

"When I said "Wait a minute," she pulled this big dagger and said she was going to kill me. She pulled it out of her purse. She said she had it for protection from bastards like me. I just took it from her and I don't know what happened after that. I guess the tables have turned. Stupid broad, how much money did I have...sixteen bucks right? Why did she want to take that too? Jesus Christ. I didn't mind paying her fifty dollars for a piece of ass, but she didn't have to try and take my last few dollars, too!"

Amanda Leigh St. John also known as Linda Peagram was pronounced dead at 10:50 p.m. on April 1, 1977 at Wellesley Hospital.

My father picks up the story from there:

* * *

Sergeant Herman Lowe and myself had been working the afternoon shift and were just getting ready to pack up and call it a night when the phone rang. The call came in around 10:40 p.m. We were the 'on-call guys' that night anyway and would rather continue working at the office than go home only to be called back.

"Better call Sheila, Herm and I'll call Jean. We've got a murder."

"So what else is new," Herman rolled his eyes, we hadn't finished the last one. It had been a busy year.

"Thank God we ate!" Herman said. "Where do we have to go?"

"Larry's Hideaway on Carlton Street. Suspect's on his way to 51."

"Where's the body?" Herm asked already making notes in his blue memo book.

"Wellesley Hospital. I'll call them right now."

I made the call to the hospital and spoke to Constable Bills. He informed me that the victim had been pronounced dead on arrival. "Stay with her, I'll send someone over," I said.

"Ready?" I asked my partner as I hung up the phone.

"Let's go," Herm answered, swigging down the last bit of coffee. We quickly completed our calls home. One more night away. Before leaving the office, I found Staff Sergeant Bill Urie typing furiously at his desk.

"Um-hum," I coughed, standing directly above him.

"Bill, I really need to get this done, I'm off in an hour," he said, not even lifting his eyes from the old Underwood.

"I know, but I just need you to do one little thing for me," I smiled.

He looked up. "One little thing? Okay, let's have it."

"We've got a body at the Wellesley. Couple of uniforms there with her, stabbing victim. Could you go over and see what you can do as far as identification? We would really appreciate it."

"Never could say no to you McCormack. So much for getting out of here on time," Urie sighed.

"Thanks, I owe you one."

"I think you owe me many!"

With that done, Herm and I were out the door of 590 Jarvis Street, heading south to Carlton Street. We got to Larry's Hideaway at about 11:00 p.m. and were met by Constable Mike Luxton and Sergeant Garry Beckett. They told us that the homicide had taken place in room 225 and the accused had already been taken to 51 Division. Herman and I proceeded down the hall to the room. Constable Shulga was standing in front of the door. I told him to remain there and keep recording the names of any person permitted to enter or leave the room including Herm and myself.

The inside of the room was a scene of destruction. Blood everywhere, on the baseboards, the light switches, pillows and bed. It looked like someone had taken buckets of it and thrown it helter skelter throughout the place. The room had a dirty look to it and smelled musty, unclean. Two officers from the Identification Bureau, Sergeant Don Nesbitt and Constable Earl Wilson had arrived and been given access to the room. They were photographing every piece of evidence and lifting fingerprints where they could. In a heap on the floor by the bed were the clothes of the deceased. Her silver coat was neatly folded on the windowsill. All blood stained, splattered. A lamp was overturned. The room looked like a battlefield.

After taking notes, we went directly to 51 Division, leaving the scene in the capable hands of the uniformed officers and the Identification officers. We got to 51 sometime after 12:30 a.m. Staff Sergeant Mel Elo was on the front desk when we walked in.

"Hi Bill, hi Herm, I'd love to welcome you, but this goddamn place is a zoo tonight and with you two here using up all my manpower, the welcome is not meant at all," he laughed, always trying to be the tough guy. "Just kidding guys, anything I can do to help, you got it. I've never seen it so busy as it is tonight."

"Okay Mel, thanks. We'll be up in the detective office, we'll give you a buzz if we need anything."

It wasn't until 1:00 a.m. that we actually had the opportunity to speak to the suspect. We entered the small room where William Willsie sat. There were three chairs, a small desk and no windows.

"Could one of you officers get me three coffees?" I asked the uniformed officers standing in the outer office.

"Sure Staff, how do you take it?" Constable Buchanan offered.

"Two double-double, what about you?" I asked the accused.

"Regular," he answered.

"Two double-doubles, one regular."

"No problem, back in a minute."

"Thanks."

Herm and I stepped inside the door. Sitting before me was an overweight, middle-aged man with thick black-rimmed glasses. His hands and wrists were covered with dried blood. For a moment I glimpsed a brief smile on his face.

"My name is Staff Sergeant McCormack and this is my partner, Sergeant Lowe, from the Toronto Police Homicide Squad. What is your name?"

Herman and I each took a chair and I pulled out my standard pad of foolscap.

"Robert Marvin Willsie," he answered. I wrote it down after checking the spelling with him.

He then provided me with his date of birth and where he was living.

"Have you been drinking tonight?" I asked.

"Yes. I don't think I'm drunk though," he answered.

"Do you work?" I asked.

"No."

I then told him he was under arrest on the charge of murder and read him the caution. I asked him if he understood. He said that he did.

"Maybe we should get you something to wear." I nodded to Herman who let out an exasperated sigh. "I'll see what I can do."

Herman left the room, returning with a typewriter and some paper. "We'll have a coat and shirt for you here in a minute," Herman said grudgingly.

"Okay, thanks," Willsie nodded.

I placed the statement form in the typewriter and began to ask questions.

"On April 1st, 1977 at about 11:00 p.m., the body of a woman who has now been identified to me as being one, Amanda Leigh St. John, was found at the Larry's Hideaway Hotel, also known as the Prince Carlton Hotel, room 225. This woman was taken to the Wellesley Hospital where she was pronounced dead. What if anything can you tell me about the circumstances of her death?" I stopped typing and waited.

Willsie's eyes went from me to Herman, then back to me again. Herman's arms were crossed in front of him. We waited.

"All I can say is I picked up a broad in the Warwick Hotel and we ended up at Larry's Hideaway and I paid her fifty bucks. She tried to steal my last fifteen dollars. When I objected to her robbing me, she got mad. On the window ledge, was a silver leather coat and from underneath it, she pulled out some kind of a dagger. She came at me, likely to do me bodily harm. To protect myself, I grabbed her by the wrist and I got the knife away from her in the battle, I don't know what to say right now, I don't know what happened after that."

We were momentarily halted by a knock at the door.

"Coffee's here." Constable Buchanan handed them to Herman.

"Okay," I continued. "Is there anything else that you wish to tell me at this time?"

"Just this. If she didn't try to rob me, this wouldn't have happened."

I noted the spray of dried blood on his arms, behind his glasses, on his forehead, his legs and upper body. "Sir, there appears to be some discoloration on your hands. Could you tell me what, if anything, that is?" I pointed to the dried blood.

"I don't know what it is," he responded.

"Is there anything else you wish to tell me?"

"No. That's it."

We finished our coffee and Herman took Willsie to the washroom. He washed his hands and spit into a paper towel. Herman gave him a shirt and coat and brought him back to the office. We handed him over to the arresting officers and left 51 Division. Our work was just beginning. It was a detailed case, one that required us to obtain several statements, gather evidence and present a case that would lead to a conviction for second degree murder, contrary to Willsie's self-defense motive. Herm and I returned to headquarters and immediately began an in-depth investigation into the background of the accused and also the background of the now deceased. Statements were obtained from everyone who attended the scene or had anything to do with Amanda St. John.

It was also customary to leave a detailed confidential report for Chief Harold Adamson so he would have it first thing in the morning. Since it was the weekend, it would be seen by one of the Deputy Chiefs. We couldn't go home until this report was finished.

As Herman and I were not very proficient two-finger typists, we both sought to use whatever charm we could in obtaining one of the most capable civilian employees from the Records department so we could dictate the report and she could type it. This became a ritual and on my appearance at the door, the supervisor in charge, Gary Rossiter would rush out of the office and protest, "Not you again McCormack, I can't spare any of my clerks."

"I promise, it won't take more than ten minutes, Gary, they'll be highly rewarded!"

"Highly rewarded my ass, we're running at minimum staff now."

"I know, I know, we are too, it's crazy out there tonight, just a few minutes, I promise."

I knew I had him when he crossed his arms over his chest and scoped out the office. "Okay," he wavered, "but only for ten minutes."

I knew it would probably be a bit longer, usually I needed them for at least two hours. Without the able assistance of the civilian employees whom we had a great rapport with, much of the investigations that were conducted could not have been possible. They were the backbone of the Police organization. We all pulled together as a team. He loaned me one of his best.

As a result of our ensuing search of Amanda St. John's apartment, several pieces of evidence were located, including a book that had no direct bearing on the murder itself but was interesting to note. She was quite a successful call girl and kept a detailed name and address book of clients complete with their likes and preferences. Some of her clients were well known members of the community, politicians, and businessmen.

It was discovered that Amanda St. John had a steady

income from these clients and there was no reason for her to engage in any other work. Hence, it would be evidentiary that the alibi of the accused was not in keeping with the deceased's financial state or character. Further, 'the book' as it then became known, contained names of some very prominent people in the Toronto area. Amanda St. John had never had any problems with the police in the past and although she plied a dangerous trade, one thing for sure, she was not a thief.

Staff Sergeant Bill Urie arrived at Wellesley Hospital shortly after 11:00 p.m. He went directly to the emergency room where he was met by Constable Larry McCoy and Constable John Bills. They told him what had happened and showed him the room where Amanda St. John's body was held. Opening the door, Bill Urie could see a stretcher with a white sheet covering the entire body.

Pulling back the sheet, he saw that it was the body of a woman, lying face down. A knife with an imitation bone handle was buried between the shoulder blades. There was an Eagle's head on the top of the handle. Blood covered the handle and the eagle's head. There was also a second wound in the back to the left of the spine, slightly lower than the knife location, but still in the upper back area. The handle of the knife was approximately four inches long.

At 11:30 p.m. that night, Doctor L. Dworatzek, the coroner on duty arrived at the Wellesley Hospital.

"What do we have here Detective?" he asked, donning a pair of latex surgical gloves.

"Stabbing victim. Knife is still there." Bill Urie pointed to the body.

Doctor Dworatzek proceeded to examine the girl. "Let's get this knife out, see what we have here."

The process of removing the knife was difficult as it was deeply imbedded in the back of the victim. This would be a crucial element to the Crown's case and to the defense who would be seeking a not-guilty verdict due to the issue of self-defense. The fact that the knife was in her back was a crucial piece of evidence that would disprove the accused claims. If Amanda had her back to him, how could he have been in fear of his life?

Once the knife was removed, Doctor Dworatzek and a nurse turned the body over for identification. Staff Sergeant Urie noted cuts on the left side of the neck, upper chest and on the back of the right arm.

Amanda Leigh St. John was taken to the morgue to await an autopsy the next day. The post-mortem examination was scheduled for 10:00 a.m. Staff Sergeant Ron Prior, who had come in to start his day shift at Homicide was detailed to attend.

"Get as much evidence as you can from the wounds, he's pleading self-defense." I instructed Ron before he left the office. It was 9:00 a.m. and Herman and I were just finishing up.

"No problem Bill, what do you especially want me to note?" Ron lifted an eyebrow. For some reason they always thought I wanted more than the obvious.

"Do I have to teach you how to do your job? The wounds man, the wounds!" I patted him on the back, following closely behind as he made his way through the outer door.

"Okay, okay. I get the picture," Ron laughed throwing his coat over his shoulder. "Get some sleep you guys." Ron knew that the notes he took at the autopsy would be presented in court and would assist the jury with the crown's version of what happened at Larry's Hideaway.

Ron Prior attended the autopsy and brought the findings back. Sergeant Don Kettle of the Identification Bureau went with him to record the proceedings. The exam was performed by Doctor Richard Hutson of the Toronto East General Hospital. Staff Sergeant Prior observed six stab wounds on the victim, front and back. Cause of death was found to be exsanguinations (loss of blood) due to stab wounds to the throat and back. Consistent with self-defense? That would be for a jury to decide.

* * *

I was seventeen when Amanda St. John was killed and I remember it well. I had just submitted my application to the Metropolitan Toronto Police, hoping to join as a cadet. After leaving 590 Jarvis Street, I walked up to Bloor Street and headed for the subway. I picked up a newspaper in the subway on the way home and read about the case. It struck me that Amanda was so pretty, not much older than me. Amanda's death caused a wave of panic amongst the prostitutes in the downtown area. They all knew the risks involved in their profession but this homicide brought it to the forefront. The last hooker killed in Toronto before Mandy was ten years previous. The murder was kept alive in the media but like anything else, with time, it settled down then disappeared.

The trial for William Robert Marvin Willsie took place on February 13, 1978 and lasted for five days. Willsie was represented by Mr. David Cousins and the Crown Attorney was Mr. Claire Lewis who would later become the Chairman of the Public Complaints Bureau. William Robert Marvin Willsie was found guilty of Second-Degree Murder and sentenced to life imprisonment.

He appealed his case and was granted an appeal in February 1981, exactly three years after his first trial took place. At the second trial, Willsie appeared before Mr. J. Osler of the Supreme Court of Ontario, his lawyer this time was

Clayton Ruby. Willsie entered a plea of not guilty to Second-Degree Murder, but guilty to the lesser offence of Manslaughter. This was agreeable to the Crown and the Defense due to the fact that the court clerk for the original trial had committed suicide prior to transcribing his notes and had destroyed his original notes from the first trial. Willsie served eighteen months in a reformatory for this crime.

This particular case was unusual because it put the population of prostitutes in the downtown area in fear. It also had a direct effect on Mandy's secret clients, many of which contacted us immediately and availed themselves of their services out of fear that their relationship with the deceased may be discovered and they would be called as a witness to court to explain that relationship. Fortunately for them, this was not to be the case. Prostitutes continue to be prime victims of murder. They are available, mostly transient and are willing to go anywhere with strangers. Many times, they are without families or friends and their disappearances go unnoticed, at least for longer periods than most. It is a dangerous but lucrative profession for some, dead end for most.

In an investigation of homicide in today's world, there are many tools available to detectives, the advancement of DNA, fluorescent fingerprint lifting and even computerized databases. The pathological examination of a deceased person and work done by pathologists is still unequalled and will always remain the main source of evidence for cause of death which is crucial in the conviction for a capital case and, females remain to this day the highest percentage of deaths by homicide. Although we have reached an age where we recognize domestic violence for what it is, it is a phenomenon that has been dissected, researched but not controlled and continues to be the leading cause of death for female homicide victims.

Murder in the first degree

"Murder is first degree murder when it is planned and deliberate. Irrespective of whether a murder is planned and deliberate on the part of any person, murder is first degree murder when the victim is a police officer."

Detective Mike Irwin, Metro Toronto Police.

CHAPTER FIVE

DEATH OF A COP

MY TEENAGE YEARS WERE UPON ME IN THE LATE 1970S and I didn't really think much about my future, what I would do with my own life, much less what my dad was doing with his. I was unaware of the painstaking hours he spent working as a detective in the Metropolitan Toronto Police Force, solving crimes, working night shifts, attending autopsies.

As I neared the end of Grade 12, I knew that I had to make a decision about my future. I was leaning toward community college and studying to become a radio-television broadcaster. I had a keen interest in music and journalism and thought this would be a good career path for me, that and the fact that two of my other friends would also be taking the course I enrolled in. Becoming a cop wasn't my first priority although it always was somewhere in the back of my mind. I finally decided to go to Centennial College that September for journalism but without my friends. They had worked over the summer and decided against going back for more education.

* * *

During that time, my father and his best friend, Sergeant Don Madigan were both on a committee of Catholic Police Officer's that organized an annual "Communion Breakfast." The breakfast was a yearly gathering of Catholic Police Officers on a chosen Sunday morning in spring. The officers went to mass at St. Michael's Cathedral, Toronto's largest Catholic Church, then over to a local hotel for breakfast. It was an event complete with roasts and speeches.

This affair was a "boys only" ordeal and had been since its inception. Maureen Madigan, Don's daughter was the same age as me and we had grown up the best of friends. We decided that we should also attend this annual event, after all, it was a year of many changes for women. When I was seventeen, Maureen and I attended our first "Communion Breakfast" with our fathers. It was an inspirational time for me. I was in the company of the two men I respected the most in the world and Maureen and I were breaking into brand new territory. It was strange to be in the company of so many men, the only two women, girls really, yet we felt completely at home. It seemed so natural. I took notice and thought about belonging to this elite group of undercover guys and uniformed officers. It was more than a gathering, it was a brotherhood and I felt a great sense of belonging here.

That summer, I went with my Dad to the "March Past" at the Canadian National Exhibition. The March Past was a highly anticipated event where the Toronto Police had officers marching in a parade for the public, highlighting the human side of our work, a grudge match tug-of-war with the Detroit Police, track and field events and demonstrations from the Emergency Task Force. Policing on profile for the education of the public.

It was here in the stands that I had my first contact with a female police officer. Sitting next to me was a beautiful young officer named Julia Kincaid. Julia was wearing the dress uniform, complete with skirt, tunic and cap. Her blond hair was pulled back into a tight bun. She was the epitome of pride. She had stature and grace and I couldn't help but openly admire her. I knew then, that I wanted to be just like her. Much to my dad's vexation, I joined the Metropolitan Toronto Police Force in April, 1980. There were only one hundred and fifty-six women on the Force and Julia was one of them. She and I became friends in the ensuing years.

There are no words that can fully describe the feelings that police officers have when paying their last respects to one of their own. Pride for the work we do, what we represent and what we have lost. Companionship and empathy with each other because we know that but for the grace of God, it could just as easily have been each and every one of us who was taken. We feel the loss of a police officer as deeply as we would feel the loss of a family member, a brother or sister.

Since becoming a police officer, I have attended eleven police funerals including one in Montreal when the first female officer in Canada was shot and killed in the mid-1980s. During this twenty-two year period, fifty-six officers have lost their lives in the line of duty in Ontario. When a police officer is killed in the line of duty, it usually is in a violent manner.

When I joined the Metropolitan Toronto Police, I was nineteen years old. The world, my life and my career were challenges that lay ahead of me and I was anxious to experience them all. I am very proud to be a police officer and I think of it as a vocation. Our family is immersed in police work. My father was the Chief of Police, I have three brothers Bill, Mike and Jamie who are all members of the Toronto Police Service. My husband Max is a Staff Sergeant with the Toronto Police, his only brother is a Toronto police officer, my brother-in-law Tony is also a serving police officer. My sister Lisa graduated from University and took the private sector route.

April 4th, 1980 was my start date with the Toronto Police. I was about to experience many changes to my lifestyle and so was my father. He was promoted to Inspector and assigned to the headquarters duty desk. I was given a uniform and assigned as a cadet to the Charles O. Bick Police College on Finch Avenue in Scarborough. I reported to the College after passing a physical, psychological and medical exam.

On my first day, I met my fellow cadet classmates. One of them was Stephen Irwin who I connected with immediately. We learned that we were both from police backgrounds, although at that time, it was just Dad and me. My brothers all joined after I did, but my grandfather had been a cop and my dad's cousin was also a cop in Toronto.

Stephen, not only had a father with Toronto Police but his two brothers, Michael and John were police officers and his sister Cathy was married to a Royal Canadian Mounted Police officer.

In those first weeks we spent together, Stephen told me the story of his father. Michael Irwin had been a detective with the Metropolitan Toronto Police when he and his partner Douglas Sinclair were shot and killed on duty on February 27, 1972. My dad had worked with Doug Sinclair and knew Mike Irwin well. Dad was in the Homicide Squad when they were killed.

Stephen and I grew very close and I have great respect for him and his family. Theirs was a tragic story and they lived the fear that we all face as police officers and relatives of cops. Steve's mom Barb has been an inspiration to me my entire adult life. She was the first police widow to fight for benefits that included cost of living clauses.

* * *

February 1972. Since the turn of the century, nineteen officers had lost their lives in the line of duty in Toronto. That was equivalent to the annual toll in some U.S. cities of similar size.

The song "American Pie" by Don McLean reached number one in the United States in 1972. It was released in 1971 and was a tribute to the late Buddy Holly. It was extraordinary how the words to this song could be applied to Stephen Irwin's own tragedy.

"But February made me shiver, with every paper I'd deliver. Bad news on the doorstep...I couldn't take one more step. I can't remember if I cried when I read about his widowed bride. But something touched me deep inside, the day, the music died..."

The day the music died for the Irwin family was on a late winter's morning in 1972, Saturday February 26th. It was cold, foggy, typical February weather for Toronto. Finishing his night shift, thirty-eight year old Detective Mike Irwin made his way home. He was tired. Mike had been on the Metropolitan Toronto Police Force for twelve years and had recently been promoted to the rank of Detective and transferred to 32 Division. He held badge number 1683.

A good-looking, tall man, his thick brown hair and dancing eyes were the first things people saw. He was a fun loving man, well liked by his fellow officers.

It had been a long night but Mike wasn't destined for bed just yet. By 8:30 a.m. that morning, he was driving two of his four kids to the barbershop for a haircut. John was twelve, Stephen eleven. His eldest son, Mike was fourteen. Mike was staying with his aunt in Unionville for the weekend and the oldest of the four, his daughter Cathy who was sixteen, was at home with her mom. The boys got their haircut while Mike leafed through some magazines. When they were all done, he drove them home. It was time for bed. He crashed at 11:00 a.m. that morning, drifting off into a well-deserved slumber.

Mike was awake shortly before 5:00 p.m. After showering and dressing, he jumped into his 1968 Pontiac station wagon and drove to the bus stop at Yonge Street and York Mills to pick up Cathy, his sixteen year old daughter and her girlfriend. Cathy had been to get her haircut that day as well, in one of the downtown salons in Toronto.

"Can we stop off at the mall for a second Dad?" Cathy asked as she climbed into the car.

"The mall? What do you need there?" Mike asked.

"I need to get a present for one of my friends."

"Sure." Mike answered and it was off to the mall where Cathy purchased a Wedgwood dish. They were home again by 6:30 p.m., just in time for dinner.

The family sat down to eat together. The Irwin's house is one of those homes that are always warm and inviting, filled with kids, friends and relatives always dropping by. It is a gathering place full of love, laughter and great food. Mike and Barb Irwin had a good life. They were young with their four kids and relished every moment they spent together. That fatal night, dinner consisted of steaks, peas and french fries. It was dinnertime for the kids but not for Mike. They spent the time talking and laughing as a family.

"That was a great breakfast!" Mike remarked, lifting an eyebrow. "It sure went down good, maybe tomorrow night we could have bacon and eggs." He winked at his wife.

"I'll see what I can do," she said as she smiled back.

After the dishes were cleaned and put away, Mike and Barb discussed the vacation they were planning for the upcoming summer. They were to take the camper to Lake Superior for a week. Mike was looking forward to this trip with the family. He bought the camper the year before and they'd already enjoyed one trip. By 7:15 p.m. that night, he was in the car once again, driving Cathy to her friend's house. Mike sat with the girl's grandparents in their living room while he waited for his daughter to have a visit with her friend. They watched the first period of the Vancouver-Toronto Hockey game. At 9:15 p.m. he drove Cathy home and watched the rest of the game. Toronto beat Vancouver 7-1.

Once the game ended, Mike switched the TV off and made his way from the living room to his son's bedroom to say goodnight to Steve and John. He tucked them into bed, running his hand through their hair as he always did.

"Good night boys, God bless," he always said, closing the door behind him. By 11:15 p.m. that night, he was dressed in his suit and ready to head in to 32 Division for the night shift. Barb walked him to the door. At the door, he turned to her and whispered:

"Bye Hon, see you in the morning.... and keep the kettle hot. I might bring some of the boys home for tea."

"No problem," Barb said. "Good night Hon, be careful."

Mike leaned down for a kiss from his wife. "Don't worry Hon, when he calls number 1683, that will be it." Mike pointed upward, a smile lighting up his face.

As she kissed her husband goodbye, Barb remembered something. "Oh, there's a couple of dollars on the table in case you're going to eat somewhere," She handed him the money.

"No thanks," Mike said, "where I'm going, I won't need it."

He closed the door behind him. They were the last words he ever spoke to her. At the time, Barb thought it was strange. It was only moments later that she remembered that Mike planned to attend the annual Police Communion Breakfast at St. Michaels Cathedral in downtown Toronto the next morning. An event for which he had already purchased his ticket.

* * *

Michael Irwin was born in Toronto in May 1933. He grew up a Catholic in the Yorkville area where he met Barb. Barb was protestant and she attended Jessie Ketchum Public School while Mike went to St. Basil's Catholic School. One thing St. Basil's didn't have then was a schoolyard so Mike went to Jessie Ketchum to play ball. Barb and Mike were thirteen when they met in the schoolyard of Jessie Ketchum Public School. They quickly became good friends and started dating when they were sixteen.

Mike went to Jarvis Collegiate in his teens. In those days, Catholic students paid tuition to attend a Catholic high school and Mike's mother didn't have the money so he went to the public school. The couple were married in September 1954 at St. Basil's Catholic Church on Bay Street. Barb was only twenty-one. Mike went to work at BNA Motors on Avenue Road as a car salesman even though his dream was to be a police officer. Mike's grandfather had been a cop in London England and his mother was not too keen on the idea of her son following in his footsteps. In 1960, Mike decided to join the Metropolitan Toronto Police Force at the age of twenty-six. He and Barb moved to North York the following year.

Thomas Douglas Sinclair (Doug) was forty-five years old in 1972. He had been a Toronto cop for twenty-three of those years and during his earlier years as a cop, he also was the part owner of a small restaurant in Keswick, Ontario. This restaurant was well known for the mouth watering butter tarts that were baked daily by a woman named Phyllis who was hired to do just that. Phyllis, the baker had a young son who wasn't sure what he wanted to do with himself after he finished school. He often went into the restaurant to have a quick bite and talk to Doug Sinclair.

When the baker's son was nineteen, Doug Sinclair eyed him thoughtfully. Sitting at the counter before him was a strong, strapping, good looking kid.

"Ever consider joining the Police Force?" Doug asked the young man.

"Not really, do you think it would be a good job?"

"I think you'd be really good at it." Doug smiled.

"Where would I be a cop?" the baker's son asked.

"How about Toronto?"

The boy turned up his nose. "Toronto, I hate Toronto. Every time I go there I get a headache."

Doug Sinclair managed to talk the lad into taking a trip down to the Metropolitan Toronto Police employment office located at 92 King Street East. Sitting across the desk from the Deputy Chief of police, the boy had two questions to answer.

The deputy asked, "How old are you?"

"Nineteen."

"Why do you want to join the Police Force?"

The young man thought for a moment. "I don't really, Doug Sinclair told me I should."

The Deputy got up from his chair, "maybe you should come back later after you think about it for a while."

As fate would have it, two years later the young man accepted Doug Sinclair's idea. That young man was David Boothby. Dave Boothby would have a magnificent career with the Metropolitan Toronto Police as a highly respected detective in the Toronto Police Homicide Squad and then succeeding my father as the Chief of the Toronto Police Force in 1995.

At 8:00 a.m., Saturday February 26, Doug Sinclair went

home after finishing the night shift at 32 Division. As soon as he walked through the door, he customarily asked his wife Ilene how she was feeling. Ilene had been a long time epilepsy sufferer. When he was satisfied that she was fine, he made his way to bed and went straight to sleep. He was up by 2:00 p.m.

It was a day of haircuts. By 3:30 p.m., Doug Sinclair, along with his wife and a lame Alsatian dog named Jasper, climbed into their 1969 Buick Wildcat and drove to a neighborhood grocery store. While Ilene was buying groceries, Doug dropped into a barbershop for a haircut even though, according to him, the feathers were getting a little light up top. The Sinclair's arrived back home by 5:30 p.m. and Ilene made sandwiches.

During this time, Bob Dzus, a young constable with the Toronto Police called to see what they were doing. Bob had been a good friend of Doug's son, Doug Junior and had admired the Senior Sinclair since he was a young lad. Doug Sinclair was quick to take Bob Dzus under his wing, identifying a need in him for an older role model. It was due to this mentoring that Bob Dzus became a Toronto cop. I worked with Bob at 52 Division during1982 and 1983. We never spoke about Doug Sinclair.

That night, after speaking to Bob, Doug Sinclair went upstairs to his den to work on his coin and stamp collection. He was a collector of many things, including hunting rifles and books. At 9:00 p.m., he turned on the TV and fell asleep on the chair. He caught a couple of hours before heading into work for the night shift. He was still asleep when his wife came in just after 11:00 p.m.

"Doug," she shook him lightly, "you're going to be late."

"Shit!" Doug woke quickly. "What time is it?"

"Just after eleven."

"I've got to go. I'm late." He got up from his chair, dressed in his suit and ran to the door. He was already in the car when he remembered something important. His gun. It was still hanging where he'd left it in the holster in his closet. He ran back into the house, grabbed the gun and yelled goodbye to his wife.

That same Saturday morning around 11:00 a.m., Lewis William Alexander Fines was just getting up. He was forty-five years old. Lewis Fines had spent his lifetime hovering between criminal pursuits and honest occupations. He had started a new job the month before as a traveling salesman in northern Ontario for the Howard Printing Company based in Toronto.

Satisfied that at last this was the job that would bring him happiness and put an end to his financial problems, he was in a fairly good mood. It was a fresh start. He and his wife Laura had four children and they were not making due with the three hundred and twenty dollars per month that he was collecting from welfare. The apartment cost him one hundred and fifty-eight dollars plus utilities each month. Lewis was behind in the rent and he owed the Hudson's Bay Company more than a thousand dollars. The Bay had already been to the apartment, repossessing the carpets, television and stereo that Fines had purchased with his Bay Credit Card.

Lewis Fines was no stranger to the police. Over a nine-year period, he had been convicted on sixteen charges ranging from auto theft, break and enter to forgery in British Columbia, and Manitoba, where Fines was born.

Well known for his forgery, he became known to police out west as "Lew the Artist." Lewis Fines served a total of eight years in jail for these offences. After serving his last sentence, he moved to Ontario in 1959 and tried to go straight.

Jack Redpath was the owner of Howard Printing. He hired Fines on a straight twelve percent commission basis after

Fines assured him he could bring in over a hundred thousand dollars a year in printing orders. Fines was known as a super con man. He was articulate, outgoing, courteous and polite. He knew how to get what he wanted out of people. Lewis Fines was up that morning by 11:00 a.m. He dressed meticulously in a suit and tie, said good-bye to his wife and kids and made his way to the Howard Printing Office on College Street. He was there for four hours, talking business with his new boss.

The meeting ended by 4:00 p.m. and Fines drove home in the 1962 gray Dodge that his employer had provided for him. He stopped at the liquor store and bought a twenty-six-ounce bottle of white rum and a large bottle of ginger ale. It was a night to celebrate. He arrived at his apartment building at 267 Roywood Drive around 5:00 p.m., took the elevator to the fourth floor and walked to the end of the hall where his apartment was situated, the last one on the left. Laura, his wife was inside with a friend.

Fines went into the bedroom where he changed from his suit to more casual attire. He was in a good mood. He came out of the room and poured a rum and ginger for himself and one for each of the women. Before drinking it, he took a shot of the white stomach medicine that had been prescribed to him for stomach problems. He sat down with his drink.

"Did you know that Sally and Roger have moved out?" Laura asked him.

"Really, when did that happen?" Lewis asked, interested now because they were supposed to have gone to a farewell party that night at the couple's apartment located just above them.

"I guess they left yesterday. They didn't tell anyone," Laura continued.

"Too bad, guess we'll just have to have our own party," Lewis remarked, pleased with the idea.

"Sounds good to me, I'll make dinner," Laura said as she headed for the kitchen.

"Nothing for me, I'm not hungry," Lewis called after her.

Lewis Fines then picked up the phone. A party would be a great way to celebrate his new job. He started calling some friends. One of whom lived across the hall. Instead of phoning, Lewis went over and asked if they would come to the party. His friend agreed.

Back in his own apartment, Laura and Lewis started to get the place ready. They replaced white light bulbs with different colored ones to add to the festive mood. To make more room, they put the dining table out on the balcony, brought out a portable bar and arranged chairs around the apartment. At about 7:30 p.m., Fines went with Laura's girlfriend to pick up another girl and on the way back, he stopped at a corner store where he purchased chips, popcorn and pop. When he got home, company was already arriving. He sent his eldest daughter across the hall to baby-sit for the couple that were attending the party.

Fines enjoyed himself, dancing, drinking, and listening to music. In fact, all was going well at the party. By 1:00 a.m. Sunday morning, the party was winding down. Some of the guests began leaving. Lewis finished dancing a polka when he suddenly started coughing. No one was sure if it was from the drinking, the exertion or the smoke in the place, but he was having a hard time catching his breath. Still, with drink in hand, he made his way to the apartment door and went out into the hall, coughing deeply.

Laura tried to follow him but he held the door shut from the outside, not allowing her to come through. The racket he was making in the hall woke his daughter who was still babysitting across the hall. She came out and saw him leaning up against the wall.

"Can I do anything for you Daddy?"

"No. Get back inside," he managed between hacks.

Laura pushed her way through the door with one of Lewis's friends. Lewis finally stopped coughing but continued leaning heavily against the wall. He covered his face with his hands.

"What's wrong?" Laura asked, concerned.

Lewis lowered his hands. His face was red, his eyes bloodshot, foggy. There was something not right, he appeared angry for no reason.

"Come back to the party," Laura said.

"I'll come back when I'm ready. Why don't you listen to me for a change?" Lewis snapped at his wife.

"Okay, I'm listening."

"In about forty five minutes, all you square johns are going to wake up," Fines said. "You and those other goddamn square johns and the law. I'm going to beat you all at your own game." Lewis threw the glass violently at the floor where it shattered into tiny pieces.

His friend asked him what was wrong and was met by a fist to the face. That was enough for him. Time to leave.

A second partygoer came to the door. Lewis waved a fist at him. It was definitely time to end this party.

Forcing his way back inside, Lewis physically pushed anyone in his path aside and went straight to the bedroom. Within a few moments, he was back out. He shoved one of the male guests, causing him to fall back on the couch. Turning, he darted back to the bedroom and slammed the door.

Inside the bedroom, Lewis Fines went to his dresser and opened a drawer. Inside he retrieved a German made semi-automatic .22 caliber rifle, Anshutz model 470 which he had purchased the previous year for sixty-six dollars and ninety-five cents. He had sawed thirteen inches off the barrel and hid the unwanted section in the hollow chrome leg of the kitchen table. He further sawed off a section of the wooden butt of the rifle, carved it into a handgrip and re-attached it to the gun. What was left was an easily concealed lethal weapon with a total length of thirteen and a half inches. The magazine held nine .22 cartridge bullets.

Fines then took an empty green plastic garbage bag from under the bed and wrapped it around the end of the barrel to muffle the sound. His other children were in the second bedroom, sleeping. The window in the master bedroom faced the Don Valley Parkway, a busy highway that connected downtown Toronto with Highway 401, the major thoroughfare in the country. Opening the window a crack, he placed the gun on the ledge and began shooting at the cars below. Four shots in all.

As the sounds of the shots echoed through the apartment, everything else came to a standstill. Laura Fines rushed to the bedroom and flung the door open where she saw her husband standing with the gun at the window.

"Put that away right now," she ordered.

"Can you hear it?" Fines asked.

"Of course we can," she stated.

"Well, it's only a cap gun," he reassured her. With that, he raised his voice so the others could hear. "It's only a cap gun," he repeated. He waited for a few seconds, then ordered her out of the room. She shut the door and returned to her guests who were all making their way out of the apartment.

The couple across the hall were deeply concerned. What started out as a fun night had suddenly turned ugly and they were worried. Returning to their apartment, they decided to call the police. They reported that the man across the hall in

Apartment 408 was shooting a rifle at vehicles. The police dispatcher said he'd send someone over right away.

Detectives Mike Irwin and Doug Sinclair arrived at 32 Division at midnight. They were partners and had been working in the detective office. Mike Irwin had been promoted in 1971, his promotion to detective confirmed only two weeks previous. It started out to be a normal shift as they sat at their desks in the empty office, completing paper work and clearing up occurrences.

At approximately 1:30 a.m. on Sunday, February 27, 1972, they got into their unmarked police vehicle and made their way to 33 Division, a short trip away in Don Mills to pick up some papers for a case. On the way, they heard the call come over the police radio. A man was firing a rifle at 267 Roywood Drive. Mike Irwin picked up the receiver to the radio and responded, advising that they were in the immediate vicinity. They would take the call. It was now 1:52 a.m.

Constable Samuel Fox was also working that night. He was a twenty-six year old uniformed patrol officer and already had ten years on the job, having started as a cadet when he was only sixteen. Sam Fox was working out of 33 Division. He was assigned a yellow fully marked patrol car and was on his own. He had just finished a call at the Inn on the Park Hotel for a fire alarm. The alarm had been false. He was ready to clear when he got another call. It was 1:48 a.m. and the dispatcher informed him that they had a report of a male firing a rifle at 267 Roywood Drive. Fox made his way to the building. He heard Detectives Irwin and Sinclair answer the call when it was put over the air for the second time. His back up was on the way.

Lewis Fines remained in his bedroom. He didn't take any more shots, instead, he took the gun and placed it back in the open dresser drawer. He then took off his shirt and put on a green turtleneck sweater, a pair of blue and white snowmobile boots and a blue nylon parka. Barging out of his bedroom, he ordered the remaining few people to "Get the hell out of here!"

Most guests made their way home but a few lingered in the hallway, discussing the change in their host. Laura Fines decided to go out to talk to them and was just opening the door when she heard her husband yell.

"Come back here!" Fines screamed at her. "I want to talk to you and I don't want any crap!"

Laura came back into the apartment and followed her husband into the bedroom. He picked up a large homemade brown leather sock-like weapon that he had filled with sand. Laura hadn't seen it before.

"Where's my gun?" He asked, confused. The gun was still in the drawer where he'd placed it.

"It's right there," Laura told him, pointing to the drawer. "It's right where you put it."

"Give it to me," Fines demanded.

Laura didn't like this. She walked over to the dresser and picked up the gun. Fines grabbed it from her hand and put it under the belt of his pants. He went through the door of the bedroom and out into the apartment. Opening the door to the hall, he saw the last of the partygoers talking amongst themselves.

"I thought I told everybody to fuck off." Lewis was very angry.

One of the men went into the apartment across the hall and closed the door. He wanted no part of this. The other two walked toward the elevators. They were a few feet away when Fines suddenly pulled out the gun and fired a bullet into the ceiling above their heads. The shot didn't appear to affect either man. Neither realized that it was a real gun, instead, they thought that Fines was playing with some sort of air gun. Fines watched them get on the elevator. He went back into his apartment and closed the door. His violent behaviour was on the increase. Once inside the apartment, he started destroying things. He kicked off the toilet seat, smashed a glass ashtray and started demolishing the stereo. He then went into the kitchen and broke a glass.

Laura Fines watched her husband silently, afraid to say anything to him. Lewis had thrown temper tantrums before and this wasn't new to her. Usually he'd wear himself out and she was sure he would this time as well.

Outside, the officers were beginning to arrive. Police Constable Fox drove north on Roywood Drive, stopping in the middle of the street outside the apartment building. He gazed out the side window of his cruiser and checked the address. Two sixty-seven. He had the right place. Detectives Irwin and Sinclair arrived at about the same time. They proceeded south on Roywood and pulled up alongside Fox.

"How's it going Sam?" Mike Irwin asked, rolling down his window.

"No complaints," Fox answered. He knew Mike Irwin, they'd worked together before in 33 Division.

"Good man," Irwin remarked. "Looks like this is the right place, let's go."

Fox parked the police car on Roywood. The two detectives drove up the driveway to the building and parked beside the main entrance. Fox met them inside the foyer. Checking the display board inside, they located the superintendent's apartment number. A new superintendent had just taken over the day before and hadn't yet posted his name on the board. Just as the officers were deciding what to do, the two men that had been at the party exited the elevator. They saw the officers in the front lobby and opened the door for them.

"I bet I know where you guys are going," one of them stated.

"What's going on?" Fox asked, determined to get some information before going any further.

"Nothing much," the man replied. "There was a party in Apartment 408 and our friend is up there shooting an air gun." The man seemed unaffected.

"What's his name?" Sinclair asked, taking out his memo book and pen.

"Fines, Lew Fines."

Constable Fox asked them both for their names and addresses and entered them in his book. He noticed their eyes were bloodshot and they both were slightly intoxicated.

"That all?" the man asked.

"For now," Fox told him.

Detective Sinclair held the front door open . "Take it easy you two," he said, watching them stroll through the door.

"The air should straighten them out," Irwin grinned. "Soon as they feel that cold they'll sober up."

With that, the officers crossed the lobby and got into the empty elevator. On the way up, Irwin introduced Fox and Sinclair. As the elevator was making the climb to the fourth floor, Lewis Fines went back to the door of his apartment and stepped out into the hall. His wife followed behind him, standing in the open doorway. Fines had had enough. He was leaving. He reached for the frosted glass fire door that lead to the stairwell beside his apartment. Unexpectedly, he turned back to the doorway of his own apartment and took out his wallet. Reaching inside, he pulled out a ten-dollar bill and handed it to his wife.

"You better take this Laura." He said.

"That's okay," she answered. "I don't need it, maybe you should keep it."

"No. Where I'm going, I won't need it." Fines answered with a tone of finality in his voice. He placed the bill in her hand and turned away. The last words he spoke to his wife were the same words Mike Irwin uttered to his own wife hours before.

"Oh my God!" Laura Fines thought to herself as she watched her husband turn away, "he's going to kill himself." She backed into the apartment, not knowing what to do.

Fines was still in front of his doorway when the officers stepped out of the elevator. At first, they didn't see him. They started down the hall toward Apartment 408. Irwin and Sinclair walked side by side, Sam Fox followed a few steps behind. Their intention was to go to the apartment and listen outside the door for a few minutes before going in. Because the men downstairs had told them that Fines was armed with only an air gun, none of the officers had their own guns drawn. Irwin and Fox still had their overcoats buttoned up.

The two detectives were approximately thirty feet from the apartment door when Fines suddenly stepped back into the hallway. He saw them coming. Instantly, he pulled out his gun.

"Okay, drop that," Irwin ordered when he saw the gun.

Fines stared at the officer. Irwin held out his hand. "You had better give that to me," he asked, coming closer.

Fines raised the gun and fired. Mike Irwin tried to turn but the bullet hit him in the left side of the head, directly above the ear. He fell backwards on the carpet. Fines shot again, two more times. The first bullet struck Detective Doug Sinclair in the chest, passing through his lung and coming to rest in his back. The second bullet ripped through his scalp, ricocheted to the right wall of the skull before exiting the left wall and coming to rest in the wooden door of a utility cupboard located in the hall.

As Doug Sinclair slumped to the floor, Sam Fox dove into the doorway of Apartment 407, the one next to the Fines Apartment. He attempted to smash the door open with his shoulder as he hit it but couldn't get the door to budge. He had approximately nine inches of cover behind the frame and he pressed himself as tightly as he could into the opening as Fines once again started shooting.

"Good God!" Fox thought, "That ain't no air gun and now he's going to kill me, too!"

Lewis Fines fired a total of five shots at Fox. He was so close that Fox could smell the gunpowder. "This is it!" Fox thought. Life was over, he felt sick to his stomach instantly.

At that precise moment, Detective Sinclair miraculously raised himself onto his left shoulder, grabbed for the gun from his holster and tore it out. Fines was a man obsessed and continued firing at Fox, not noticing the wounded officer on the floor. Sinclair mustered up all the strength he had left in him and managed to fire one shot at Fines. The bullet smashed through the frosted glass section of the fire door at the end of the hall, directly behind Fines, causing him to panic. He turned around and pushed the door open, running through it. As he made his way through the door, Sinclair fired two more times, missing Fines completely. Sinclair fell back to the carpet, coughing up blood. Fines took the stairs two at a time, escaping down the stairwell.

Constable Fox didn't know what to do. Instantly, he was out of the doorframe, pausing momentarily by the two detectives. He could hear Doug Sinclair whispering.

"Get your gun out son," the dying detective told him.

Fox had the .38 special in his hand. His hand was shaking. Cautiously, he went through the fire door and hesitated, peering over the railing. Fines was running down the stairs, he already had a two-floor advantage. Fox aimed his gun, no clear view. He had to chase him.

Douglas Sinclair was mortally wounded. He knew both he and his partner needed help right away. Rolling over to his stomach, he started crawling, covering the thirty-foot distance along the carpet toward Lewis Fine's apartment. As he inched slowly forward, his lungs began filling up with blood. Mike Irwin was unconscious on the floor behind him.

Fox reached the second landing. Pausing momentarily, he took a second to catch his breath, his heart pounding relentlessly in his throat. He could hear nothing from below. Silence. Fines must have stopped. Constable Fox waited, straining to hear, not daring to make a sound himself. The clicking sound of a gun pierced the calm, immediately sending a chill up Fox's back. Fines was re-loading. The sound was unmistakable. Fox could hear the cartridges hit the floor as Fines dropped them in his attempt to load as quickly as possible.

Fox screamed at the gunman. "Give up! You're surrounded! Do you hear me?"

There was no response. Only silence, then one distinct sound. Fines was shooting again. The sound of the bullet echoed through the stairway. It hit the spot directly under Fox. The smell of gunpowder filled the air once again. His pulse was racing so hard that Fox was sure the gunman could hear it.

Fox remained silent, afraid to move, then he heard the footsteps start up again. As he listened, he heard them further below, then the sound of a door opening and closing. Fox made his way down the final flight of stairs. A brown leather wallet lay open on the second step from the bottom. He picked it up and put it in his jacket pocket.

Guardedly, he landed at the bottom of the stairwell, sweating profusely, heart pounding so hard he was sure it would come straight through his chest. He took a quick look under the crawl space beneath the stairs. Empty, save for two cartridges lying askew on the floor. The fire door faced him. He had to go through it. Slowly, he pushed the door open. A long concrete corridor lay before him. It was empty.

Two lone light bulbs illuminated the corridor. Graffiti was plastered over both sides of the concrete walls. A closed door lay at the end. Another obstacle. It was like a bad dream enveloping him, would this ever end? He pushed open the next door, only to find another empty corridor. At the end of this corridor, there was an open passageway that lead to the left. Noiselessly, he made his way to the passageway, ever mindful that Fines had the full advantage. It was the perfect set up for an ambush.

Fox reached the corner and deciding it would be suicide to turn into the passageway, he decided to go back the way he came. The two detectives needed his assistance. He got back to the fourth floor, nearly tripping over Doug Sinclair as he came through the shattered fire door. Detective Sinclair had made it to Fine's apartment and was now lying just inside the doorway. A second uniformed officer, Edward O'Donohoe had arrived on the scene after a frantic phone call from a tenant in one of the other apartments had been made to the Toronto Police in which they advised that an officer had been shot.

Constable Craig Worsfold arrived a few minutes later.

"Get your guns!" Fox screamed when he saw the officers. "The guy who just shot Mike and Sinclair is still out there, he may be in the building!"

The two officers had their guns in their hands. One knelt down beside Irwin. Fox bent down over Sinclair. Sinclair coughed. Fox yelled to O'Donohoe. "Get over here, he's still alive!"

O'Donohoe raced to Sinclair's side.

"Keep him on his side and make sure he keeps breathing," Fox told him.

"Irwin's alive too," O'Donohoe stated.

Fox nodded, "We'd better move then." He knew he had to get them help right away. He went into the Fines apartment. Laura Fines was in the living room. She looked up, panic-stricken.

"What's happened?" she asked the officer, noticing the gun in his hand. "Where's my husband?"

"Where's your phone?" Fox asked impatiently, ignoring her question.

Laura Fines pointed to a phone on a table beside the wall. Fox called for an ambulance, then phoned 33 Division where he told the desk Sergeant what had happened. Hanging up, he asked Laura Fines for some cloths. She ran into the bathroom and returned with two wet facecloths. Fox took them from her and went to Sinclair. Wiping the blood from his face, Fox started mouth-to-mouth resuscitation. Sinclair was coughing blood. Fox didn't know what to do next. He ran back into the apartment and phoned North York General Hospital.

"Get ready for two emergency ambulance cases!" he yelled excitedly into the receiver.

Hanging up the phone, he went back to see what he could do with Sinclair. It was now 2:20 a.m.

Approximately half an hour earlier, at 1:50 a.m., Constable Donald Penrose of 33 Division was investigating a traffic accident on the Don Valley Parkway when he heard the emergency call on his radio, for an officer down. He was finished with the accident and he ran quickly to his cruiser and raced toward the scene. It took him ten minutes to get to the apartment and when he arrived, he saw Fox's yellow cruiser parked on the street. Penrose decided to pull into the driveway and parked behind the unmarked police vehicle.

Penrose was unaware of what had transpired in the building. He radioed the dispatcher and asked what they wanted him to do. The dispatcher told him to stay where he was and remain on the air.

Lewis Fines was still on the run. In fact, he hadn't waited in the open passageway to ambush Fox but instead followed another passage that brought him into the front lobby where he went out the front door. By this time, information had been broadcasted to the other officers in the area about the suspect and his description. He was to be considered armed and dangerous.

Constable Penrose was now standing beside his cruiser. He saw a man in a blue nylon parka come through the front entrance and head down the sidewalk towards where he was standing. The man was carrying a dark object that Penrose couldn't make out. As the man neared his location, Penrose took out his gun.

"Okay, hold it right there," he demanded, pointing to his .38 Smith and Wesson revolver directly at the man. Fines did what he was told.

"Now raise your hands," Penrose ordered.

Fines slipped the rifle into his left hand, holding it close to his body. He lifted his right hand into the air.

Penrose saw the gun. "Drop it! And get both your hands up."

Fines was in no mood to obey orders. He dropped his right hand and was now clutching the rifle tightly with both hands.

Penrose raised his revolver. "Do what I tell you!" He yelled.

Fines took off. He crouched down in front of Irwin and

Sinclair's unmarked car. Penrose took a position of cover behind his own car and waited, listening for movement. There was none for a few seconds, then, Penrose heard the man running. He was heading toward the back of the building, disappearing into the darkness.

Jamming his gun back into his holster, Penrose went for the car. He drove it across the laneway, effectively blocking it off. Calling the dispatcher, he asked for further assistance and gave a description of Fines over the radio. O'Donohoe arrived on the scene and Penrose told him what had happened. O'Donohoe headed inside to see if he could be of any assistance. Penrose went out on foot, making his way down the laneway, checking parked cars along the way. The man in the blue parka had disappeared.

Fines wasn't finished with his mission yet. After making his way to the rear of the building, he found an open door and let himself in. Returning to the crawl space under the main floor stairwell, he paused for a few minutes, checking over his weapon, then re-traced his steps back to the front lobby. Getting on the elevator, he got off on the third floor and headed toward the stairwell. A tenant in one of the apartments on the third floor heard someone run past his doorway toward the rear staircase. He looked out in time to see a man in a blue parka heading for the stairs.

Constable Fox was beside himself. He had just finished calling the hospital and returned to render any assistance he possibly could to Doug Sinclair. He was kneeling down beside the dying officer when he heard the steps on the staircase behind him.

"Someone's coming!" Fox whispered to the other two uniformed officers. The three of them cocked their guns. Sam Fox stood up, turned around and opened the fire door that separated him from the stairwell. At that moment, Lewis Fines stepped onto the landing between the two floors and faced him.

Fox stared unbelieving. "Stay right there!" he ordered.

For a few seconds the two men stared at each other, neither of them moving. Fines had the rifle behind his back in his left hand. Fox could see the barrel sticking out between Fine's legs.

"Drop the gun! Do it now!" Fox yelled.

Lewis Fines refused to move.

"Drop your gun," Fox repeated.

Fines continued to stare, unmoving.

Constable Fox fired three times. The first bullet hit Fines in the chest, the second through the neck and the third above the right ear, lodging in his skull. Fines was dead when he hit the floor. Sam Fox was sure Fines was dead. He walked down the six steps and picked up the gun. He then walked back up to the apartment where Fines had lived and called 33 Division to tell them what had happened.

Laura Fines was in the apartment. She heard the shots. "What happened?" she asked. She was standing near the doorway.

"You'd better go and sit down," Fox told her. She remained standing. It was then that she noticed her husband's rifle in the officer's hand.

"Is Lew dead?" she asked.

"Go and sit down," Fox ordered. "Sit down, or I'll have to handcuff you."

"I'm okay," Laura stated. She turned and went into the bedroom.

The reinforcements arrived. In a matter of minutes, the entire place was swarming with cops, uniformed and plain-clothes. One detective made his way into the apartment and saw Fox still gripping Fine's gun. "Why are you holding that son?" He asked.

"I'm not sure how to safely unload it," Fox told him.

"Sit down Sam," the Detective said, gently taking the rifle from the young officer's hand.

Fox sat on the sofa. The gravity of the entire situation struck him then. It was overwhelming, surreal.

Outside the apartment, an ambulance crew strapped Michael Irwin to the stretcher and made an emergency run to North York General. He was still alive, barely clinging to life. A second ambulance crew arrived. They took Douglas Sinclair together in the same ambulance with Lewis Fines. Both were declared vital signs absent, dead on arrival to hospital.

A few blocks away from the scene, most of the Irwin family was sleeping, unaware of the events that had transpired. Another Toronto officer, Detective Sergeant Rod Marsh was Mike Irwin's brother-in-law. He was married to Barb Irwin's older sister June. At 2:40 a.m. that morning he awoke to the sound of his telephone ringing. The phone ringing at that ungodly hour was never a good sign for a cop. The call came from police headquarters. The news was grim. Mike Irwin had been shot. Rod Marsh got dressed and made his way to the Irwin's home. He rang the bell. Barb Irwin and her eldest daughter Cathy were just getting ready to go to bed when the doorbell rang. Barb answered the door. She saw Rod standing at the entrance to her home and knew right away.

"I knew it was you," she said.

"There's been an accident Barbara," he stated, lowering his eyes.

"Oh Rod," she said, "I had a feeling. I felt all night that something had happened."

"Get your stuff, I'll take you to the hospital."

"Should I tell the kids where I'm going?" she asked, unsure of what to do.

"It's okay Mom, I'm here. Let them sleep," Cathy reassured her.

"Let them sleep Barb, we'd better get going," Rod said.

They drove directly to St. Michaels Hospital where Mike had been rushed by ambulance as North York General was not equipped to deal with his injury. On the way to the hospital, Barb and Rod passed right by the apartment building where Mike had been shot. Rod Marsh didn't know it was so close to their home until he saw all the police cars out front on Roywood.

Stephen was awake. He had heard the doorbell and the conversation that had taken place. Out of fear, he didn't get up until his mother and uncle had left. Once she was gone, he went down stairs.

"What's going on?" he asked his sister.

"I'm not sure. Dad's been in some kind of an accident. I don't know anything more than that." Cathy looked very worried.

"Should we wake John up?" Stephen asked.

"I think so."

Stephen and Cathy woke up their sleeping brother and the three of them went back downstairs. They turned on the radio where reports of the shooting were just coming through. Detective Doug Sinclair was dead. So was the shooter, Lewis Fines. Mike Irwin was in hospital with a gunshot wound to the head.

They all knew this was serious. Their dad had been in a motor vehicle accident a few years before where he was the passenger in a police car when it struck another car. Mike Irwin went through the front windshield. He received several stitches to both sides of his head. This wasn't the same. They knew that this was far more serious.

Constable Rick Purdy was sent to the Irwin's home to pick up the kids. He took them to their Uncle Rod and Aunt June's house where they listened to every news report on the radio throughout the remainder of that night, the next morning and into the afternoon. They stopped listening when their mom arrived at the house. They knew it was bad news.

* * *

Michael Irwin Junior had been at his Aunt Helen's house in Unionville. He was told about the accident and Aunt Helen's son in law, Bob Syer came to pick him up and took him to St. Michael's hospital. He got there shortly after his mother and waited with her while the doctors valiantly attempted to save Mike Irwin's life. Mike Irwin lived for a period of twelve hours, he never regained consciousness. Barb prayed to God for time to sort out what it was she was going to do. In that period of time, her prayers were answered and she looked past her grief, realizing her purpose in life. She had to be strong. She had to raise her four children.

Michael Irwin died at 2:05 a.m., February 27, 1972. He was born in St. Michael's Hospital in 1933. He died in St. Michael's Hospital in 1972. That morning, he was to have attended at the annual Police Communion Breakfast at St. Michael's Cathedral. St. Michael is the patron saint of police officers.

As with any shooting, murder or killing, whether it is police or civilian, the homicide squad is called in to conduct the investigation. My dad was not on call the night Mike Irwin and Doug Sinclair were murdered. Detective Bill Kerr and Detective Sergeant John Leybourne were. They answered the call at 3:30 a.m. that morning and made their way to the scene. They were fighting hard to get rid of the shock. Doug Sinclair had been a good friend of theirs.

When they arrived at the scene, they made their way to the fourth floor where they were met by Chief Harold Adamson. His face was ashen.

"You men are in charge of this investigation. Do your best," he told them, knowing full well that it would be hell investigating the death of a friend. Chief Adamson left the scene. He had to see Ilene Sinclair first, then Barb Irwin.

The two detectives surveyed the scene, noting the chalk outlines where the officers had lain. Sam Fox was still in Apartment 408. He was seated on the sofa when they came in. He was obviously in a state of shock.

"Let's get him out of here," Bill Kerr stated.

They made arrangements to have him taken home. Then they went to work. It was a painstaking job, taking measurements, photographs, collecting evidence, bullets, casings, keys and wallets as well as guns from the fallen officers. Leybourne carried Fine's rifle to a window, pointed it toward the ground outside and pulled back the bolt. A single cartridge ejected from the chamber. Leybourne then removed the clip. One cartridge left. Two lethal shots, had Fines taken them.

Laura Fines cooperated with the police. She turned over a full box of .22 caliber cartridges that she found under the bed and a further thirty-six rounds that Lewis Fines had loose in a plastic bag. The detectives also found two letters written by Lewis Fines in a drawer. These letters indicated that Fines had planned an act of destruction and had every intention of carrying it out.

At 7:45 a.m. that morning, the two detectives drove to the North York General Hospital. They made the identification of Detective Douglas Sinclair. Lewis Fines body was in a separate room. The detectives found a rifle clip holding five cartridges in one of his pockets. They then had to attend the autopsy for Doug Sinclair. It was 2:10 p.m. Sunday afternoon. It would be one of the most difficult tasks either man would ever have to face in their careers as police officers. After the autopsy, they received a call from a nun at St. Michael's Hospital. Michael Irwin had passed away. They were on their way to St. Mike's immediately.

The letters that Lewis Fines had written described him as a troubled individual who was deeply in debt. He planned a violent caper, hoping that he would be killed during it so that his wife and kids could have a clean start. There would be no reasoning with him.

This was one case, my dad was glad he didn't have. Although the following year, he would be involved in the investigation of another police officer killed in the line of duty, Constable Leslie Maitland.

My father remembers the day Irwin and Sinclair were killed. It was one of those horrible moments in a cop's life that he never forgets. These were his friends, colleagues. Dad has a vivid recollection of what he was doing that day:

I was in the Homicide Squad that year but I wasn't on call that weekend. On Sunday February 27, 1972, I got up around 7:30 a.m. to get ready for the Communion Breakfast. Mike Irwin had been involved with the Communion Breakfast for years and that was mostly how I knew him. Kevin Boyd picked me up and we were on the way downtown when we heard the news over the radio. We couldn't believe it. Kevin and I were both in shock.

We went right to headquarters and asked what we could do. There was nothing. It was done. We were told to go ahead to the Communion Breakfast. We made our way to St Michael's Cathedral. It was the saddest mass I'd ever been to. We prayed for Mike Irwin, for Doug Sinclair and their families. We were all deeply affected.

I had worked with Doug Sinclair when he was in the General Assignment Squad. I actually worked with him as his partner for a few weeks in old 57 Division at 135 Davenport Road. Doug Sinclair was a well-dressed, handsome man. He was the epitome of the "Hollywood detective." He often carried his revolver in his pocket and told us 'always have your gun in your pocket with your finger on the trigger guard whenever you go to any call.'

He was the last person I would ever have thought would get shot. Mike Irwin was a terrific guy, he was always in a good mood, a real family man. I met him when he was in the old 7 Division. He worked with Kevin Boyd. Kevin was killed in a car accident in 1980.

* * *

The funeral for Michael Irwin was held at Annunciation Catholic Church on March 1, 1972. It was a bitter cold day, freezing rain and miserable. Father Bill Harding was the priest who conducted the service as he had been an instrumental person in the Irwin's lives. Barb Irwin became a Catholic in 1965 and Father Harding was the priest who had confirmed her. He had a brother named Dave who was also a priest. Father Dave Harding baptized my kids, married my brother Mike and my sister-in-law Liz and was a great friend to my mother, Jean.

168 • KATHY CARTER

When Father Bill Harding died, I was in full uniform and assisted with the funeral procession by escorting the hearse from the church to his final resting place at Holy Cross Cemetery. I was truly honored to be able to pay my respects to Father Bill by assisting. He had been a rock for the Irwin family and helped them through this terrible, tragic time. He was a friend to my family and truly a man of God.

Michael Irwin and Douglas Sinclair were buried in two separate Toronto cemeteries. Both officers were awarded, posthumously, the Medal of Honor. This is the highest award the police department presents to an officer. Mike Irwin was also awarded the Robert Kennedy Award for police heroism, an award that has rarely been presented on an officer outside of the United States.

On March 02, 1972, Lewis Fines was cremated in the Toronto Crematorium at his wife's request. His ashes were placed in a plastic container and buried in common ground behind the crematorium. There is nothing to mark the site.

The widows of the dead detectives each received life insurance and money from the police association's Widows and Orphan's funds. Barbara Irwin had two teen-age children and two young children to raise on her own. She received Mike's salary with no increase. Barb Irwin became an advocate for the right to have a cost of living brought into effect for widows of slain officers. She petitioned the Police Commission headed at that time by Charles O. Bick. She was met with constant roadblocks. Disgusted and frustrated, she appeared on a television show in the early seventies called the "Schulman File."

Doctor Morty Schulman was the interviewer and he also wrote a column in a popular Toronto Newspaper. He also had his law degree. Barb Irwin appeared on the show with Edward Greenspan, one of Toronto's most famous and influential criminal lawyer's. Morty Schulman was appalled at the lack of support given to widows financially. As a result of all her hard work, the Police Commission under the direction of His Honor Judge Phil Givens decided in Barb's favor and agreed to add a cost of living increase for widows, however, it was not retroactive. The first widow to benefit from this was Karen Sweet in 1980. Her husband Michael Sweet was killed in the line of duty that same year.

Day to day, year to year, decade-to-decade things change, people change, circumstances change, relationships change. We meet people along the way that influence us, harden us and move us. In so many ways, we are all interwoven, our lives connecting, crisscrossing on our life maps.

The week before he was killed, Mike Irwin was grocery shopping with his wife when he saw Lewis Fines in the same store and pointed him out to her.

"See that guy over there?" he asked Barb as she loaded up the cart with food for their growing family.

"Yes, what about him?"

"I know him. There's a warrant for him out west." Mike answered, always on duty.

"You know everyone," Barb laughed not thinking that this man who now stood across from her in a simple checkout line would be the one to brutally kill him, complete irony.

Samuel Fox continues to serve the public of Ontario as a police officer and has had a long and distinguished career. Stephen and John Irwin are serving members of the Toronto Police Force. Michael Junior left the Toronto Police Force and joined the Ontario Provincial Police. From there, he took a full time position at the Ontario Police College and is now retired. Cathy is still married to Mike, an RCMP officer. She works as a civilian for Toronto Police as does one of her two daughters, Catherine. The other, Michelle, continued on in the Irwin tradition and is a Constable for the Toronto Police Service. I stood through her graduation ceremony at the Toronto Police College with her two uncles, Stephen and John and we watched her receive her shiny new badge from Chief Julian Fantino.

I thought of the supreme sacrifice her grandfather had made, how undeterred this courageous kid was, this courageous family are ... and the moment her father, complete in RCMP red regalia kissed her cheek, I was overcome with pride not only for Michelle but for the profession we share.

If you look out the front door of the Irwin's house, you can see 267 Roywood Drive, the place that Mike was killed. It is literally a stone's throw away. Their street runs directly off Roywood Drive. The apartment building where Mike lost his life stands erect, hovering directly over the rooftops, ever there to remind them and us all of how fragile life really is.

EPILOGUE

I have been a police officer for twenty-two years. I took some time off when I had my two girls, but I know I could never leave policing for good. It's in my blood and that of my family. My father retired from the Toronto Police Service after serving over thirty-five years. He became the Chief of Police which is a fantastic achievement. Researching this book has brought me back to what veteran officers now refer to as "the good old days." I have had an opportunity to revisit many of my dad's cases and speak to so many officers he worked with and who I worked with, in one capacity or other, and who my brothers and husband worked with.

Although we have investigated many deaths and misadventures, none of us were fortunate enough to join the homicide squad, which has to be the one regret I have.

Police Officers are a well-linked, well-connected brotherhood. We are somewhat incestuous at times, being very protective of each other, mostly because of what we experience together everyday – the tragic events of other people's lives, the destruction of property, lives lost. We develop a strange sense of humor, one that helps us get through the day. What I have learned from this journey is that every instance in one's life is important. One decision, one action, irrational or rational that any one of us make at any moment can affect so many others, change futures, destinies.

In December 2002, a very special friend of mine, a Crown Attorney from the Scarborough Courts, Arleen Goss passed away after a lengthy battle with cancer. She was a fighter, both in the courts and in her own personal life, time after time, beating the odds until at last the odds beat her. She had just turned 40. I flew to her funeral in St. John's Newfoundland with Vanessa, one of my best cop friends. It was Christmas time, the bustle and hustle of life going on all around us and yet here we were, taking the time out to pay our respects at yet another loss of life, a young, talented person taken in the prime of her life. How quickly life is taken from us, how great and fragile a gift we are given, every second, every minute, every day that we can spend with the people we love counts for so much.

There are some who believe in pre-destination. I believe that certain actions, once set in motion can cause diverse outcomes, good and bad. "VSA," vital signs absent is used universally by emergency workers, ambulance, police and fire departments. "10-45" is the Police code in Ontario, Canada, for death. It simply means a dead body whether by misadventure, homicide, accidental or natural. It is a code that immediately sparks fear, anxiety and doubt, for the dead cannot speak, but the circumstances around a death can sometimes tell a truly amazing story.

ABOUT THE AUTHOR

White Knight welcomes to its round table of talent a new author with her first book on true crime. Kathy McCormack Carter is no newcomer to writing having previously developed two works of fiction that await publication. Her natural aptitude to do great research shows in the fine crafting of the stories herein.

McCormack Carter is not a newcomer to police work having been born into a police family that goes back generations into Ireland. Her father, William J. McCormack, author of two books, was highly regarded as a recent Chief of Police of Metropolitan Toronto, and remains so today.

Because I have personally know the McCormack family since the 1970s, I have the opportunity to honestly and openly salute the type of service the McCormacks continue to provide.

I hope you will take the time to understand and respect what compels a person to choose police work as a career, having to face the dangers that abound on the street in this unpredictable, drug-saturated society.

Kathy McCormack Carter loves her work serving the public, and now as a writer, and member of the Crime Writers of Canada, her second career begins to unfold in this book.

Bill Belfontaine, Publisher

White Knight's Remarkable Women series

In keeping with White Knight Publication's mandate to bring great titles of social concern to book and library shelves across North America, I am indeed fortunate as publisher to have been closely involved with the latest publications in White Knight's "Remarkable Women Series" listed below.

Conscious Women — Conscious Lives

A unique book that lives up to expectations that women across North America constantly provide the nurturing component that continues to make our countries so great. These stories from across Canada and the United States of America, bring home those concerns that women have for other women providing love, nourishment and hope for our present and future generations. Remarkable women, everyone.
ISBN 0-9734186-1-3   216 pages
PB US $13.95 Cdn $19.95

Sharing MS

This informative book by the author and two women friends with Multiple Sclerosis, is a beacon of common sense lighting the way of those who have MS or suspect they may be afflicted, as well as being helpful to family, friends and health professionals. Read the book then call the MS Society Chapter in your local telephone book for information about your concerns regarding Multiple Sclerosis.
ISBN 0-9730949-7-4   218 pages
PB US $13.95 Cdn $19.95

The Unusual Life and Times of Nancy Ford-Inman

This story is about a most remarkable woman who contributed so much to Britain's literature, the theatre, media and the war effort in spite of a major physical handicap. Badly crippled by Cerebral Palsy at an early age yet she fought her way to become the author of almost 60 romantic novels and journalistic endeavors too numerous to count.
ISBN 0-9730949-8-2   238 pages
PB US $13.95 Cdn $19.95

Genres of White Knight Publications

Biography
*The Life and Times of
Nancy Ford-Inman*
– Nancy Erb Kee

Gay Adoption
A Swim Against The Tide
– David R.I. McKinstry

Inspiration – Self Help
*Conscious Women –
    Conscious Lives*
– Darlene Montgomery
Sharing MS (Multiple Sclerosis)
 – Linda Ironside
Sue Kenney's My Camino
– Sue Kenney

Personal Finances
*Don't Borrow Money
    Until You Read This Book*
– Paul Counter

Poetry
Two Voices – A Circle of Love
– Serena Williamson Andrew

Politics
Turning Points – Ray Argyle

Self-help
Books by Dr. K. Sohail
• *Love, Sex and Marriage*
• *The Art of Living
    in Your Green Zone*
• *The Art of Loving
    in Your Green Zone*
• *The Art of Working
    in Your Green Zone*

True Crime – Police
"10-45" Spells Death
– Kathy McCormack Carter
Life on Homicide
– Former Toronto Police Chief
Bill McCormack
The Myth of The Chosen One
– Dr. K. Sohail

**Recommended reading from
other publishers**

History
An Amicable Friendship
– Jan Th. J. Krijff

Religion
*From Islam to Secular
    Humanism* – Dr. K. Sohail
Gabriel's Dragon
    – Arch Priest Fr. Antony
    Gabriel
Pro Deo
    – Prof Ronald M Smith